The Ultimate Guide to Horse Health & Care

The Novice Owner's Guide to Horsekeeping

LAINEY CULLEN-MCCONKEY

Skyhorse Publishing

Skyhorse Publishing books may be purchased in bulk at special discounts for sales promotion, corporate gifts, fund-raising, or educational purposes. Special editions can also be created to specifications. For details, contact the Special Sales Department, Skyhorse Publishing, 307 West 36th Street, 11th Floor, New York, NY 10018 or info@skyhorsepublishing.com.

Skyhorse® and Skyhorse Publishing® are registered trademarks of Skyhorse Publishing, Inc.®, a Delaware corporation.

Visit our website at www.skyhorsepublishing.com.

10 9 8 7 6 5 4 3 2

Library of Congress Cataloging-in-Publication Data is available on file.

Cover design by Daniel Brount
Cover photograph by gettyimages

Print ISBN: 978-1-5107-4527-8
Ebook ISBN: 978-1-5107-4528-5

Printed in China

With thanks to the wonderful professionals and friends who kindly looked over this book and made helpful suggestions.

Your input and advice were greatly appreciated:

Anne Shaw
Janet Dallimore
Tara Hill
Diane Elyard
Ericca Hoffman
Susan Donaldson (MRCVS)
Dr. Fay O Herrero (DVM)
Dimitri Delgado, Delgado Prized Arabians

Any and all errors in this book are mine, not theirs!

Contents

About the Author

THIS is always the hardest part to write.

About me. Well, I started riding when I was around fourteen, and very soon started helping out at the stables. This led to a more formal equine education as one of my first trainers told me she wanted me to start working on my "stages." This was way back before the Internet, so I didn't even really know what that was, but "stages" were the formal British Horse Society examinations in horse care. I started to learn the intricacies of horses and their care, and I've been learning that ever since.

Fast forward almost thirty years to now, and I own my own small boarding stable where I look after three horses of my own (a Quarter Horse, a Thoroughbred, and the Thoroughbred's son, an APHA colt we bred ourselves) as well as a number of boarded horses. I try to keep my equine knowledge current by keeping up on new research and participating in online seminars as well as the daily education provided by the horses under my care.

I am also owned by two dogs, four cats, three turtles, thirteen parakeets, ten chickens, and an unknown number of tropical fishes, and of course, my rock, my husband, who puts up with all my craziness.

Foreword

So, you've decided to take the giant step of keeping your horse at home, on your own property. It can be as wonderful and idyllic as it sounds, but there are also a lot of things which need to be taken into consideration to make sure you (and your horse's new home) are ready for this! Of course, if you've been a horse owner for a while, you may already be accustomed to many of the topics covered in this book, but it never hurts to have a reminder! Over the past few years, I have encountered a number of lovely people who have made the decision to keep their own horses at home with very little practical experience, and I have come to the conclusion that a book giving some sensible guidance may be useful for people in this situation. It is my hope that this book will offer some understanding and advice as you take the leap.

It is a daunting thought, that you will be wholly responsible for the health and wellbeing of a large animal like a horse, but always remember that even though horses can be subject to serious (and potentially expensive) problems, the vast majority of horses are remarkably easy to manage, provided you take care of the basics. This book isn't meant to be a textbook, but rather a handy guide from the viewpoint of a horse owner, trainer, and caretaker. Over the last thirty or so years I have learned an awful lot about the trials and tribulations of horse care, and I hope that this book will help you avoid some of the more common pitfalls and worries. The subjects covered here are certainly not exhaustive, so please do keep reading and researching as you go through your horse care journey. Think of this book as a sort of printed version of the "helpful, more experienced person" you encounter at most boarding barns.

Always keep this in mind: the only *stupid* question is the one you *don't* ask! Your vets/farriers etc. are there to take care of your horse, but they're not mind readers. If you want to know something, ask them! Also, as an aside, please try to learn as much as possible, from books and practical experience or training, but also use some common sense. I once had a girl who wanted to come out and "help" at our facility, without any experience. I explained that I did not have the free time to train someone unless that training was part of a lesson program, and her response was "It's okay, I don't need any training. I watch a TV show where they run a boarding barn, so I know what to do!" Ahh . . . no. (I remember watching an old episode of a show called *Renegade* where one of the main characters said that a horse had died from colic, because they found evidence of that in the horse's brain. Again, no!) While watching videos produced for training and education purposes certainly has a lot of value, you cannot assume that a TV show is going to give you accurate information.

Chapter 1

A Home Fit for a Horse

Because let's face it, they're more important than kings!

THE ideal home for a horse is, of course, free roaming over acres and acres of rolling pasture. This, however, is rarely possible, especially when you want to keep your horse at home. The proper home will also vary somewhat depending on the individual horse and their workload. A

show horse, for example, couldn't reasonably live in the same place as a child's Shetland pony, since their needs (admittedly dictated by our desired activity) are quite different.

Ideally though, every horse should have access to daily turnout, for exercise but also for mental health. Horses are flight animals and being cooped up in even the nicest of stalls is stressful for them. The general rule of thumb for area required is about one to one and a half acres per horse.

Pasture Care/Management

Fencing and water, along with grass type/quality are the most important factors to consider when looking at pasture. Fencing can be comprised of many different materials, but must above all be safe and in good repair and a minimum of four feet high.

The traditional post-and-rail fencing, with at least three rails, looks very nice but does require regular maintenance, i.e. checking for damaged/broken areas as well as painting or otherwise treating the wood. Even wood which has been pressure treated will require painting. These days, you can buy PVC post-and-rail fencing, which will not need to be painted or treated but simply pressure washed occasionally to keep it looking nice. However, the posts on this type of fencing are actually just sleeves that cover regular wooden posts, which are susceptible to rotting, and as they are covered it may be hard to check them.

If you don't want the expense of post and rail, you could go with post and wire. The wire needs to be strung tightly and should be the same height as rails would be. Some people are very against barbed wire, but I've never had a problem as long as the wire is correctly tensioned. I've given myself more cuts with it than I've ever seen on our horses! The alternative is smooth wire, of course, or you can use mesh wire, the "no-climb" type for horses in which the squares are too small to trap hooves. If you like, for appearance as well as security, a top rail can be installed with your preferred wire below. When installing *any* kind of horse fencing, though, the boards/wires should always be attached from the pasture side. That way, when a horse decides to use the fence as a scratching post, they won't be so likely to push the fencing right off the posts.

The other common type of horse fencing is electric fencing, either bare "hot" wire or tape style. This can be useful if you have a horse who constantly leans on or over the fence. Just attach the wire inside the fence on insulators so that they hit that before the actual fence. Otherwise, though, I would really only use electric fencing as a temporary barrier, perhaps to temporarily split the pasture. I do know people who use it as their main containment within a larger area, but my personal preference is for a more permanent physical barrier. In the end, the type of fencing used is less important than ensuring that it remains safe and secure. Fences should be checked regularly (weekly) and a proactive approach should be taken regarding maintenance.

Keep in mind that horses are very picky, wasteful grazers, and they will eat the "good" grass while leaving weeds untouched. In a perfect world, we would split our grazing area into at least three separate paddocks, and use a rotational grazing system. In effect, one pasture is being grazed by your horses; the second is being cross-grazed by cattle, sheep, or goats; while the third is being rested and allowed to grow. Pasture management varies widely depending on where you live, but not many of us are fortunate enough to have sufficient pasture area to do this. For example, in Florida it can be hard to keep decent grazing as the climate isn't ideal for good pasture grasses. Summer brings lots of heat and sunshine, but also lots, and I mean lots, of rain. Winter is the dry season, and the combination of low rainfall and shorter days has a great impact on grass quality and growth. If at all possible, try to split your grazing into at least two sections to allow half to be rested at a time.

Something else you must keep in mind is that grass is a pretty delicate plant, and if the roots are damaged, the grass won't grow. Horses have sharp hooves, and if they are turned out on a wet pasture, they *will* damage the grass. If you constantly turn them out in soaked pastures, you will soon find that the field (particularly around the gate area) will become poached into nothing but a sea of mud! Not only is this slippery (well, slippery for horses but *great* at sucking a pair of rain boots off your feet!), but it can also encourage infection in any small cuts your horse may have, so if you have a prolonged period of very wet weather, you may need to keep your horse confined to a stall (or at the very least sacrifice a section of your pasture to protect the rest).

The most basic of pasture care/management is keeping the pasture clean, so at least once a week get out there and scoop the poop! There are two reasons for this. First, horses don't like to eat around manure, so those areas will become rank and unappetizing to your horses. Second, keeping the pasture clean will help a great deal with parasite management. This is also why cross-grazing can be very helpful, as other animals will ingest horse parasites/eggs/larvae without any harm (except to the parasites), and so help to clean your pasture.

Some people recommend dragging a harrow across the pasture, breaking up and spreading the manure as a natural fertilizer. This should only be done on a hot, dry day as this will kill off any parasites in the manure. Done on a wet or humid day, it could have the opposite result and you would effectively be seeding your whole pasture with parasites. Of course, the other drawback of this is that you need the equipment to do the job, so unless you already have a harrow (and something suitable to drag it with) good old-fashioned people power will get the job done. All you need is a wheelbarrow and muck fork and a little time. Bonus: you get to spend a couple of hours out with your horse, just observing them and enjoying their company while getting a bit of a workout yourself.

Housing

We'd all love a beautiful barn with large stalls, nicely concreted aisle, and perfect tack and feed rooms with lights and fans and all the other bells and whistles. Our horses, on the other hand, will be quite happy with a shelter which lets them get out of the wind and rain (or snow/sun, depending on your location). Also, farriers and

vets do appreciate and deserve somewhere out of the elements to do their work, so a field shelter can also serve this purpose.

If you are on a tight budget, building a three-sided "run-in" shed is probably the cheapest and easiest option. Three walls and a roof, with the open side facing away from the prevailing wind if possible. The open side should be one of the longer sides so that horses can enter and exit easily. (This will also reduce the chances of a horse being trapped in there by another horse if you have more than one). The shelter should be large enough to hold all your horses and needs to be of sturdy enough construction to withstand weather conditions and also horse damage from kicking.

It is a good idea, if possible, to have some method of enclosing all or part of such a shelter, so that a horse can be kept in there if necessary due to injury, illness, or simply convenience, i.e. not having to go searching for them when the vet or farrier arrives.

There are many ready-to-assemble stable blocks available in a wide range of designs, from a single stable to multiple stables with attached tack and feed rooms. The only real limits are your budget and available space. Think of it from your horse's point of view, would they prefer a modest stable with lots of grazing area or a super-duper fancy stabling area with lots of spare stalls . . . and a postage-stamp-sized pasture? I'm sure you know the answer! Another consideration is whether you need any planning permits or the like, which vary widely by country/state/county. So before getting too deep into planning a building project, a check of local rules and regulations will help avoid any problems. Design and construction of stabling is a subject which could fill a book all by itself, so I'm going to leave it at that. Basically, if all you want is a field shelter/run-in shed, that would be fairly easy to construct yourself. For more traditional stabling, the prefabricated, ready-to-build (or indeed, having someone build it for you) is probably the easiest way to go, though maybe not the cheapest. But if local rules say you need permissions, the builder will often deal with this headache for you.

If you choose to stable your horse at night (or during the day as some prefer in warm climates) then you will also need to consider appropriate bedding material as well as disposal of manure and dirty bedding. The traditional bedding of straw can be quite hard to come by, not to mention the potential for a bored or greedy horse to eat their bed (though this can be discouraged by sprinkling with disinfectant).

Straw breaks down more readily than wood shavings, the other common bedding material, but straw is also bulkier to store and dispose of. I would suggest that shavings are probably the easiest way to go, particularly if you buy the vacuum-packed, dust-extracted bagged shavings. They are quite easy to store, as they are wrapped in plastic, and being compressed they don't take up a huge amount of storage space. You can also use shredded paper products and pelleted compressed sawdust, but like most things you must balance convenience and cost. Another option is to use special rubber mat flooring in the stalls, where you need only put down a very light covering of shavings (many horses don't like to pee on the mats as it splashes onto their legs). This is expensive at the outset due to the cost of the mats, but it does drastically reduce the amount of shavings which will be needed and also make stall cleaning quite easy.

Disposal of manure should be as far from the stabling as practical. If possible, the best idea is to have a small dumpster solely used for manure that is emptied regularly. If this is not feasible, you could try asking local plant nurseries and the like if they can use some free organic fertilizer. If you have no option but to have a traditional muck heap, it should be as far from other buildings as possible, as the rotting process generates considerable heat. You should also try to make sure that it isn't likely to contaminate any local water sources. The old-fashioned "ideal" was a three-section muck heap. One section in use, one section rotting down, one section completely rotted down and being removed/used as fertilizer.

Water

The most basic necessity for any animal is water. If you are lucky enough to have a river or stream running through your property, this may be all you need, but even then, there are a few important considerations. If a stream has a sandy bottom, you run the risk of sand being stirred up into the water by the horses and then being swallowed with each mouthful of water. This can lead to sand colic, which is *not* something we want to happen. If this is the case, the stream should be fenced off to keep the horses away, and you will have to provide an alternative water supply.

The other major consideration if you have a natural source of water is what is upstream of your property? Look into whether there is any chance of industrial pollutants entering the water before it reaches your property, as your horses would then be drinking pollutants. Even if the water doesn't look or smell bad, there could be chemicals or even minerals present that may be toxic to horses. For the same reason, if you are downstream of any large-scale farming areas, there could be run-off from fertilizers or herbicides/pesticides entering the water, which could again be harmful. If in doubt, for your horse's welfare, *always* err on the side of caution, even if it means a bit of extra work for you. Would you rather fill water troughs daily with a hose or have your horse made sick (or worse) because of something you could have prevented?

Ponds may also not be a good water source as they could be stagnant and have "bad" water. I have found that large ponds tend to be okay. Our property has no agriculture or industry around and our pond is larger with fish and plants to help keep it clean, but if the water is scummy or covered with algae, I would fence it off. In general, though, horses will not drink "bad" water unless they are extremely thirsty, so making sure they always have access to fresh, clean water will go a long way to preventing them from sampling anything potentially dubious.

If you are providing an artificial water source, there are a few options. You could use buckets attached to the fence or set inside old tires to prevent horses from knocking them over. These will, however, require emptying, cleaning, and refilling regularly as well as frequent monitoring to ensure your horse is never without access to water. Another option is a water trough, which can either be filled manually via a hose or fitted with a self-filling system similar to that in a toilet cistern. These are very simple and reliable, requiring only minimal maintenance. A water pipe or heavy-duty hose would need to be permanently attached to the trough, and you will need to ensure that there is some way of shutting off the water to allow for the trough to be emptied out and cleaned periodically.

If you are in a cold climate, you will need to check your water troughs etc. in the winter to make sure they haven't frozen over. Any exposed pipes/hoses will also need to be insulated against freezing. To prevent troughs freezing, the old-fashioned remedy was to float a small soccer ball in the water as it would move around and prevent the surface from freezing. These days, you can buy electric heaters which either wrap around a bucket or sit in a trough, and these keep the water temperature above freezing (this also means that you need electricity run to wherever your water is). Whatever method you choose, the important thing is that your horses have access to fresh water at all times. If on any occasion you go to feed your horse and find that they are without water, make sure to fill the bucket/trough then wait a few minutes before giving their grain ration, so that if they are very thirsty, they drink before eating.

The old rule of "water before feeding" comes from the days when horses spent their nights in stalls, without access to water, and in the morning the first job of the grooms was to lead them out to the main trough so they could drink before they were fed. The thinking was that if the horse ate their grain then drank a lot it could wash the feed through their stomach before it was ready to go further into the digestive tract (I won't go into the whole digestive system here, though). I'm honestly not sure what science there is behind this, but it seems a very simple thing to make sure the horse has water before feed, so why take the chance of causing a preventable problem?

To summarize, these are the most basic of things needed to provide a safe, healthy home for your horse.

- Safely fenced pasture
- Safe, appropriate shelter or stable
- Fresh water

Riding Area/Use of Space

If you only intend to trail ride, whether in the area around your property or further afield, then a riding area won't be much of a concern. If, however, you want to ride in an arena setting, particularly if you ride dressage, then this is something you need to plan out. If you have a limited amount of grazing land, it doesn't make sense to fence off an area and put down sand or some other type of surfacing. Not only will it cut down on grazing, but it is expensive and like everything else will require regular maintenance. I recommend laying out your arena, either 20m x 40m or 20m x 60m if you have space, on the most level area you have. Mark out the arena size and shape, then use 1" PVC pipes to form rails at the corners and a couple of points along each side/end. Sink maybe a foot of pipe into the ground, leaving another 6" sticking up, fit a 90° elbow joint, then insert a piece of pipe (I think ours came in 8' lengths) horizontally. Another sunken pipe with an elbow at the other end and, voila, a rail. Tip: do *not* glue the joints together. That way, if (when!) the horses mess with them, the joints will come apart without any damage and can easily be rebuilt. You can then use portable dressage markers, whether you splurge on the metal ones or buy the cone type or even make your own. Just make sure the markers are in the correct positions, and you're ready to ride. Bonus point: without an actual fence line to follow, you and your horse will *have* to learn to ride straight lines!

Though not exactly related to the use of space, consider whether you are likely to be riding your horse while no one else is around. Often when I ride, I am the only one home, which means that if I do have a bad fall, I could be left waiting for a considerable time before anyone even knows I have been injured. I strongly suggest that if you *do* ride when home alone, you should alert someone (spouse/parent/friend) who is in the area before you start your ride. Let them know you're going to ride and for how long. If you're headed out on the trails, tell them where you plan to go. Then, let them know when you are finished. Yes, I often forget to send the second "okay, all done and still alive" message, but my husband will then text *me* to check that all is okay. But at least I know that if I don't respond to that text, he will try again, and then doubtless head home to find out what has happened.

Always with horses, think safety first! Even the safest, most levelheaded of horses can be spooked, and even the best rider can take an awkward fall (my own trainer recently took a fall where she landed on a metal mounting block, turning a "minor" fall from a spooked horse into broken ribs and a trip to hospital).

Storage

Consider where you plan to store feed, hay, and bedding. The feed room should, ideally, have or be close to a water point to allow for handwashing, and damping of feeds. The easiest thing is usually just to build or buy a small shed. If you can run power to it for lighting, that would be good, but it isn't essential. With a little planning and thought, even a small shed will make a good feed/hay room. The important thing is to make it as rodent-proof as possible. Rats are resourceful and clever little creatures, and will very quickly eat through plastic, so invest in steel trash cans to store your feed (they aren't all that much more expensive, especially when you consider their far longer lifespan). If you empty the bags of feed into the cans to make scooping easier, make sure you do not refill the can until all the feed is gone. If you make a habit of refilling partly used cans, you will soon find that the bottom few inches of feed have spoiled and are wasted. If you are concerned about feed spoiling due to local climate, some people will install a small air conditioning unit to maintain a constant temperature. If that is a concern, I recommend just buying your feed a week at a time. If your horse has good pasture available, hay requirements will be low, so you won't be storing hundreds of bales.

Chapter 2

Essential Equipment

As all horse owners know, there is an endless list of things we "need" for our horse, but let's just talk about the stuff that really *is* essential. (Note: No matter how hard we try to make the case, that gorgeous sparkly browband or saddle pad in *just* the right shade of purple are *not* essentials! At least that was what my husband said when the new bridle arrived with the crystal browband and padded noseband . . . though in my defense it *was* on sale!)

You will already have many of these horse essentials if you keep a horse at a boarding facility, but in case you are really jumping in with both feet and keeping your very first horse at home, let's run through those, too.

Here are the true essentials for keeping your horse at home.

- **Wheelbarrow:** The two-wheeled types are more stable and easier to use.
- **Muck forks:** Yes, plural. They break, trust me, so try to have a spare on hand. The type depends a little on the bedding you use. For shavings and other fine bedding materials, you want a shavings fork. They come in metal or plastic. I suggest plastic as they don't rust and the metal tines have a tendency to bend. Remember, if a muck fork breaks, you can replace just the head on most types (the ones with a plastic head and wooden

handle). Also, even if it loses a tine, it is still fine for poop-scooping in the pasture. If you use straw bedding, you'll want an old-fashioned metal pitchfork with four or five tines.

- **Feed bins:** You can use trash cans for this, but I recommend spending a little bit extra to get steel cans to prevent rodents from chewing their way in (trust me, they chew through plastic *very* easily). For convenience, I prefer one can for each type of feed used, but if space is limited you can fit two sacks of different feed into one can (though obviously the feed will have to remain in the bag and not be dumped into the can)!

- **Feed scoops:** There's a variety of types available, so choose ones you like best. Feed should always be measured by weight, not volume, so once you know what weight you need you can really use anything to do the actual scooping. I've known people to use old coffee cans or tall plastic cups. You can even repurpose an empty juice jug by cutting off the bottom.

- **Feed buckets/skips:** Again, a wide variety of options from shallow rubber feed pans to wall-mounted mangers. I like to use floor buckets (the shallow rubber pans) as they allow for a more natural eating position. They are also easy to wash and carry, and rubber isn't as susceptible to splitting or cracking when your horse stands on it. If your horse likes to paw at their bucket and spill their feed, then you could use a wall-mounted manger or one which hangs over the stall door or fence board. Another option, if you do want that more natural position, is to find an old tire and sit the feed bucket in the tire at feeding time so that if your horse does paw, they will hit the tire and not knock over the bucket.

- **Buckets:** You can never have too many buckets. Even if you use a trough or automatic waterer, keep a couple of buckets on hand. They're not very expensive and come in handy for all sorts of things: water (obviously); soaking alfalfa cubes or beet pulp; tack cleaning; tail washing; soaking dirty bandages . . . get the idea? No such thing as "too many" buckets. Oh, and rather than buying them at the feed store, they are usually cheaper at a hardware store. Basically, as soon as you add the word "horse" to an item, it becomes more expensive! But a bucket is a bucket is a bucket, and horses truly don't care what color they are.

- **First aid kit:** We'll look deeper into this in a later chapter.
- **Halter and lead ropes:** Because, well, see bucket comment above. Keeping a couple of spares is always a good idea. There are so many kinds of halters these days that it's hard to keep up, but the cheapest is usually nylon. Now, if you plan to leave a halter on your horse all the time (even if only during the settling-in period) then you really should go with leather or nylon with a breakaway head piece. While nylon is cheap, strong, durable, and comes in so many cool colors and patterns, the thing that nylon halters don't do is break. And if your horse somehow gets their halter caught on a fence/tree/gate/leg (yes, that has been known to happen!), then you *want* that halter to break. Far better to break a halter than have your horse seriously injure itself struggling to get free. Leather will break whereas nylon will simply stretch.
- **Grooming kit:** Another minefield of "must-haves" that really are *not* necessary. A basic grooming kit should contain: rubber curry (for scrubbing off mud/dead hair); body brush (for brushing the body, in case you hadn't figured that out); metal curry comb (for cleaning the body brush, though the rubber one will also do that job); dandy brush (stiffer brush for getting mud etc. off legs); mane/tail brush (here it really is worth investing in a good one, as human hairbrushes just don't stand up to the workload—my personal favorite is the Oster mane/tail brush); hoof pick (preferably the type with brush attached). I would say that those are the truly essential pieces. Some people will insist on using a tiny face brush with nice soft bristles,

but I've honestly never found them to be of any real use. As for storing/carrying your grooming kit, you can buy totes and bags and boxes and . . . or why not just use one of those spare buckets? Told you they were useful. In the "old days" we were told to have small sponges in our grooming kit to clean eyes, nostrils, and underneath the tail (different sponges for each area, obviously). These days I just buy a jumbo pack of baby wipes. They're gentle and disposable, and as a bonus, baby wipes are an absolute *must-have* for horse shows! You can use them to wipe over horses, tack, boots, as well as cleaning yourself up if necessary. They take off dust and leave everything looking great, and for a fraction of the cost of those special tack/coat shine wipes!

- **Tack:** This is another thing you will already have if you already own a horse, but in case you don't, you will need a saddle, bridle, and bit (unless of course your horse uses a bitless bridle), plus a couple of saddle pads. If you are only just getting the horse, find out from the seller what size saddle, bridle, and bit as well as type of bit. There is such a huge variety of tack available in both English and Western styles that I'm not going to get into that. I recommend having a couple saddle pads to allow for laundering. I do *not*, however, believe in using "special" pads "to make the saddle fit." If it doesn't fit, it doesn't fit! My only concession on this is if the horse has been out of work for a while and the long muscles along the spine have weakened/atrophied a little. In this case (as with one of my own horses) I may *temporarily* use a half-pad to "fill in the gap" and keep the saddle clear of the spine. This, however, should be monitored and if after a few weeks no change is seen then the saddle itself needs to be addressed. If you're getting into using riser pads (front or rear) or wither relief pads, *the saddle does not fit the horse!* I once knew a girl with a saddle that didn't fit her or her horse. She purchased the saddle before finding a horse and insisted on using it because "it's a great quality, very expensive saddle." Which it was. Just not for that horse. I switched her to one of my saddles and, lo and behold, all of the horse's behavioral issues when ridden went away. (For someone who wasn't going to get into the whole tack subject I've done a great job, huh? I promise to stop now.)

Now that we've covered the basics, let's take a quick look at a few more items which aren't really necessities but are certainly good to have. Chief of these would be tack racks.

- **Tack racks:** You *can* store your tack on the floor, which is why I didn't put this as a true *necessity*, but tack racks can be quite inexpensive and are certainly more convenient. If you have the space and your horse is right at your house, I would recommend storing tack in your house since this is an area which will likely have the most controlled temperature. Outside tack rooms can be damp or humid, which can encourage growth of mold and mildew on leather, not to mention that you don't want rats chewing on your tack.

- **Bridle hangers:** These can be used for bridles, halters, ropes, etc., and the plastic ones are very resilient against weather, so are ideal for outside use. You can even make your own by screwing pieces of wood to the wall (think round "slices" about two to three inches thick and maybe four inches in diameter, like slices from a fence post). I have also known people to use clean tin cans of around that size, though cans these days really aren't of substantial enough construction to stand up to this use. All you want is something rounded and large enough to hold the bridle securely without creasing the leather, so avoid hooks for long-term bridle storage.

- **Saddle racks:** These come in a wide range of styles and materials. The wall mounted types are good as they keep the floor clear, but you need to make sure they are securely anchored to the wall, especially when you consider that a Western saddle can weigh up to 50 pounds (though most trail saddles will weigh in at around 25 pounds). Saddle racks can be metal, plastic, or wood of varying designs. You can also make your own wooden ones quite easily. I worked at a barn where we had an entire wall with poles running the length of the room and the saddles were lined up along those. Stable and inexpensive. Of course, only really necessary when you have to store forty or so saddles, so probably a bit more than the private owner needs. Freestanding saddle racks are also good (especially when you clean your saddle).

- **Rugs/blankets/sheets:** Whatever you want to call them. Horsey pj's if you like. Something else I'm putting here in the "not necessities but good to have" section. The need for these is obviously dependent upon where you live and also how your horse lives and what they are needed for, but the basic rule of thumb was always that if you needed to body clip your horse to make it easier to work them and prevent overheating/sweating in winter, then you would need to provide an artificial layer when they weren't working. Blankets come in a wide range of styles and weights, so it really depends on what your horse actually needs. I would rather see a horse just a little chilly in the morning when I go out than find them sweating under a blanket. You can find stable blankets for indoors and outdoors, waterproof blankets (obviously for outdoors), combination indoor/outdoor blankets, belly-covering blankets, neck covers, and . . . get the picture? The most important thing to bear in mind is that your horse doesn't *care* what color the blanket is, or what you spent on it. They *will* destroy them. They *will* catch them on fences and rip them. But the bigger problem is that if your horse is left unsupervised for long periods, they could get tangled up in a blanket if the straps come undone (which they do). I have just recently had to stitch all the straps back onto a blanket because the horse wearing it broke out of their stall and went tearing around the field wearing the blanket as a bib. Fortunately, she wasn't hurt, but the blanket was pretty seriously injured! So, if at all possible, if you aren't around, I would try to steer clear of blanketing your horse if they are turned out. Nature does a really good job at providing a horse with the warmth they need (though very young or old or unwell horses may need a bit more help). If your horse does wear a blanket, it needs to be checked regularly and also taken off regularly to check for blanket rubs, etc. Just one other point on blankets. If you don't already have blankets and need to buy them, they are usually sized in inches. To measure your horse for a blanket, measure from the center of the chest to the point of buttock (you'll probably find this easier with help, unless you're like one of those Stretch Armstrong dolls!). If you measure an odd number of inches, I would round up to the next one (i.e. a measurement of seventy-one inches would get a seventy-two-inch blanket).

- **Horse trailer:** Buying a horse trailer can vary wildly in cost, depending on size and condition. The type of hitch must be your first criterion, and this will very much depend on what type of vehicle you are using to haul the trailer. If you are using an SUV or similar, you will need to use a bumper pull hitch. If you have a pickup or other large truck you may be able to use a gooseneck, which connects in the truck bed. Always make sure that the hitch fitted to your vehicle is of the appropriate "class" for safe hauling, and that your vehicle can safely haul a loaded trailer. For this information, consult your vehicle's manual or ask a professional. The last thing you want is for your hitch to break while you are hauling your horse! If your vehicle does not already have specialized trailer brakes fitted, you should have this done before hauling a trailer. Simply put, this system makes sure that your trailer's brakes activate when you press the brake pedal, so that the trailer slows itself rather than relying on your vehicle to slow both pieces of the puzzle. Used trailers are cheaper than buying new, but unless you are very experienced with mechanical things, I would recommend having a used trailer checked out by a professional for safety before using. If you are only planning to use the trailer for local trips to shows or for an emergency trip to a veterinary hospital (hopefully not), then a small bumper pull will likely be all you need. Even brand new, these can be purchased for a fairly reasonable price. Trailer care and maintenance are covered in a later chapter, but if you do decide to buy your own trailer, make sure it is kept in good condition and ready to be used at all times. No point in having a colic emergency and finding out at three in the morning that your trailer has bad brakes! Another option is to either rent a trailer when you need one or pay someone to haul your horse for you. If you rent a trailer to haul yourself, make sure you are renting from a reputable person whose trailer is in good condition, and that you have the correct size of ball on your hitch for the trailer. This information is usually stamped on the tongue of the trailer hitch. If you are paying a professional hauler, make sure their equipment appears safe and that they have commercial insurance to haul horses.

Chapter 3

What to Know Before
You Bring Home Baby

WHETHER you have already been boarding your horse or are only just getting a horse, there are a few things you need to know before taking over responsibility for their care. The biggest thing you need to understand is the level of responsibility you are taking on. You probably think you're already accustomed to the responsibility if you've been boarding a horse somewhere for a while, but keeping your horse at home, at least if you plan to do it in a conscientious way, is going to make some major changes to your daily routine. Really, to your life in general.

Feeding Regime

Horses thrive on routine, so if your job means that during the work week you are feeding them at 6:30 a.m. and 6:30 p.m., you should make every effort to keep as close to those times on weekends/holidays too! Just because you don't have to go to work, you can no longer enjoy the luxury of lounging in bed until you feel like getting up, you still have horses who expect to be fed around 6:30 a.m. (though at least on weekends you can go back to bed after feeding). Now, I'm not saying you have to keep your schedule to the minute, but it's unfair, and bad for their digestive system and overall mental wellbeing, to feed at 6:30 a.m. Monday through Friday and then 9:00 a.m. on Saturday and Sunday. Likewise, if you are going out for the day, you either need to plan to be home in time to feed them around the same time as usual or have someone who is able (and willing) to do that for you. Do people make their horses just "live with it" and feed them when convenient for *them*? Sure, of course they do, and I'm sure most horses survive that just fine. What I'm trying to say is that you should plan your routine in a way that works best for you *and* your horse. Keeping your horse *happy* will help keep your horse *healthy*, and that's really the goal.

Now, I am assuming that your horse's current diet is appropriate for their workload and that their body condition is good. In this case, your horse should stay on their current feeding regime unless you are moving somewhere that you simply cannot source the current feed. If you already own the horse, you should be quite aware of their feeding regime, and better stable managers will have kept you informed if changes were needed (i.e., if your horse was getting fat, they should have discussed with you, then made appropriate changes). Likewise, if your horse was becoming difficult to ride/ handle, then the manager should have taken your comments on board and adjusted their diet. As an aside, if you do *not* keep your horse at home but at a boarding facility, you should *never* feel that you are not allowed input on your horse's care and feeding. A good stable manager will always discuss your horse's care with you and should be willing (and able!) to explain their thought process in making (or not making) changes. For example, if you feel your pony is a little on the thin side, a good manager would never say "He's fine, I know what I'm doing," or something similar. A good manager would agree, remind you that your pony has a history of laminitis, and that the vet recommended keeping him a little leaner than would be considered usual. (And when I was put in this very situation, I gave the pony owner, also the barn owner, a detailed and scientifically written explanation of the pony's actual dietary/nutritional requirements at his size and level of work, showing that the pony was at correct bodyweight and feed level. I also told him I would be happy to increase the amount of feed to the level "someone" had told him appropriate, but that I would require his instruction *in writing*, acknowledging that he had been warned of the health risks but wanted to proceed regardless. Needless to say, I was told to leave things as they stood. The lesson? Whether you are horse owner or stable manager, if you know you are right, stand your ground for the wellbeing of the animal!) So, it is important to know exactly what your horse is currently being fed, by weight, not volume. Yes, when we feed each day, we give the grain by scoops, but this is done for ease. The actual feed calculation is done by weight. This will be covered more fully in a later chapter, but feed scoop sizes/capacities vary, so once you know the weight currently being fed it's simple enough to use a kitchen scale to weigh out the correct amount and then pour into your scoop to see the level. And it doesn't need to be exact to a fraction of an ounce, a close approximation is good enough. If your feed level falls between markings on the scoop, then making a quick line with a permanent marker will give you an easy visual reference. Over time, though, you will be able to tell by feel if the amount you've scooped is correct.

Type of grain, amount of grain, and also type and amount of hay (unless you have sufficient good quality pasture and hay isn't needed) are important. If you are *not* able to source the current grain, you should purchase enough for a couple of weeks before moving your horse, and locally source another type with the closest nutritional match. If necessary, bring the label from the current grain to your local feed store and have them help you choose one they carry which has the same (or close to the same) levels of protein, fiber, and fat. There are many, *many* other things on the label, but those are the three I generally try to match as they have the greatest effect on the horse.

Vets and Farriers

If you already own the horse, you will be aware of their vaccination and deworming schedule, both of which should of course be up to date. If you are just buying the horse, this is information you should get from the seller. Another thing to ask the seller is when the horse's teeth were last checked/floated and their last farrier visit. If you're going to keep the horse fairly close to its old home, hopefully you will be able to keep the same vet and farrier. While the vet is very important, I would make sure to get a farrier sorted out first. After all, hopefully you'll only need to have a vet out once or twice a year, while you'll be seeing your farrier at least every six weeks! If you do need to find a new farrier, I suggest doing so as soon as possible (even before you move the horse) as good farriers in particular can be hard to find; the good ones usually have pretty full client lists. If you're moving to a new area, ask other horse owners or at the feed and tack stores to get recommendations on farriers, and don't be afraid to switch if you are unhappy with their work. I saw a really cool shirt which said: If you think hiring a good farrier is expensive, try hiring a bad one! And it's very true. That old adage of "no foot, no horse" is there for a reason, and that's why personal recommendations are so important.

While on the subject of vets and farriers, please remember that these professionals do generally require you to be there when they come out to do their work! Vets in particular often have emergency call-outs, so consider your appointment time to be a guide only, and make sure that you are going to be available on the appointment date. Often farriers and vets are not available for routine appointments on weekends either, so you need to be aware that you will likely have to make time during the week for these visits.

Something else to consider is who else is around your property. Even if they have no real horse knowledge, if you are going to be gone for large parts of the day, it is very useful to have a friendly neighbor or relative who can keep an eye out. Horses are *very* talented at getting into mischief but much less talented at getting out of it unhurt, so having someone around who can watch for anything untoward is very valuable. If you're moving to a new area, it's worth getting to know your neighbors in case you need any help in that way. Our own neighbor recently came to check if I knew our front gate was open, which I did (I was waiting for the equine dentist to arrive), but it is very reassuring to know that he watches over our property, too.

I strongly recommend that you make your very last task each night, before you head to bed, to go out and check on your horses. Far better to take a few minutes to go and look and make sure they are where they should be and seem okay than to assume all is well. If your horses are right at your house, it will only take a few minutes of your time. And one of the great things about horses is they don't care what you look like, so go out in your pajamas if you like, or your bathrobe, or whatever else seems appropriate (so far, my own best winter outfit was a fuzzy bathrobe topped with a thick padded vest, snazzily accessorized with a fleece headband and rain boots). Also, trust your gut. If you have a sudden, unexplainable urge to go check on your horse, *do it*. Yes, everything is probably just fine, but at least this way you won't stay awake wondering. There have been a number of times

I've heard sustained bouts of kicking and gone out to check whether some-one was colicky or just cast in their stall (stuck lying down). In every case (so far) it was just my lovely Quarter Horse mare being her usual cow-faced grumpy self. But that doesn't mean next time I hear it I won't go check anyway!

Rescue/Malnourished Horses

The sad truth is that too many people seem to see horses (and other animals) as disposable items, and a great many horses find themselves at auction pens, potentially headed to slaughter. There are a lot of very well-meaning people who rescue these horses, so I decided I would include a few brief thoughts on the additional difficulties of dealing with horses in poor condition.

I'm certainly not trying to dissuade anyone from rescuing a horse, but you need to be aware that many rescued horses are very underweight and/or have some kind of illness. If you already have a horse on your property and are adding a rescued horse, *please, **please*** make sure you follow all quarantine protocols! Even a horse who doesn't appear sick may be carrying strangles or another communicable disease. Hopefully your current horse would already be up to date on all of their vaccines, but why take the chance of exposing them? (And be aware that no vaccine is truly infallible.) I strongly suggest that you send the rescue horse to a proper quarantine facility for the required period (usually three weeks). Of course, they could still be a carrier of strangles and remain symptom free, but that can be said about any horse. The other major consideration is that the horse may be in very poor condition and underweight. I definitely recommend making your vet aware that you've taken on a rescue horse, and have them come out to check the horse at the first opportunity (no, not "next time they're out," but as soon as possible after you get the horse home)!

As well as starting any needed vaccinations (assuming the horse's condition is good enough that they can be vaccinated), take your vet's advice on how to best and most safely add weight to your new horse. (Hint: the answer is probably lots of good quality hay and patience.) Do not expect to fatten a horse up in a few weeks. Be patient and do things as your vet advises. Also, don't be afraid to get in touch with a nutritionist at your feed company (the actual manufacturer of your feed if you like) and get their advice.

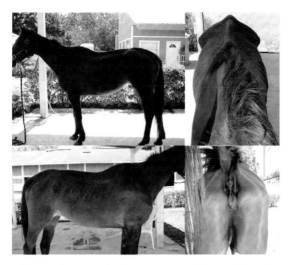

These photographs show my own Thoroughbred mare when I first met her, back in 2011. She stands at 16.2 hands high and at this time weighed 845 pounds (her correct weight is around 1,200 pounds).

This photograph was taken last week. She is now twenty-five years old but certainly doesn't look it!

Chapter 4

Feeding: Need, Not Greed

HORSE feeding and nutrition can be an incredibly complex subject, but fortunately one that is well covered in many books. The simplest thing for an owner who is new to keeping their horse at home is to just follow the horse's current feeding regime. This causes the least stress to the horse's digestive system and, if the horse is in good condition and performing well, is clearly appropriate.

As mentioned earlier, it may be the case that it isn't possible to source the exact brand and type of feed in your area, which will mean you have to make changes. In this case, there are a few things which should be taken into account. Let's assume that your horse is already on an appropriate feeding regime. You need to find out exactly what they are being fed each day, brand and type of feed, and, more importantly, *how much* per feeding. This needs to be measured by weight, not by volume, so if the person currently in charge of feeding tells you "a half scoop" or whatever, the easiest thing is to pour a half scoop into a plastic baggie and weigh it. This particularly matters if you're having to change brands of feed, as all feeds are not the same weight.

Now, if you're going to be able to keep using the same feed, that's really all you need to know. If your scoops are different from those used by the current barn, you should weigh out the feed and pour into your scoop to see the level. I don't know anyone, though, who weighs their feeds every time, so once you have the level on your scoop, I suggest drawing a guide line on the scoop with a marker or pen. By the time the line wears off, you'll have a feel for the correct amount. (And if you're feeding more than one horse and the amounts are different, they each get their own line.)

Calculating Your Horse's Bodyweight

The recommended feeding amount is what is deemed to be "appetite level," which is around 2.5 percent of bodyweight per day. To calculate body-weight, you can use a weight tape or calculate it yourself using the following Milner and Hewitt equation, formulated in 1969. Note that measurements must be taken in inches.

$$(\text{heart girth}^2 \text{ x body length}) \div 330 = \text{weight in pounds}$$

Heart girth: Measure around the horse, with the tape over the highest part of the wither and as close behind the elbow as possible.

Body length: Measure from point of shoulder to point of buttock.

I have used both methods and found that they give pretty similar results, so if you don't feel like doing the math, just get yourself a weight tape and follow the instructions. Of course, the most accurate way to calculate bodyweight is to take your horse to a weigh station. Some mobile equine vets also use a "crush" which has a horse-sized scale built right in. But for purposes of feed calculation, you really don't need it accurate to the pound. Just as a guideline, the correct feeding amount for a 1,000-pound horse would be around twenty-five pounds of feed per day. As I said, though, I don't want to get too deeply into the science of feeding. If you are interested in learning more, I highly recommend the book *Horse Nutrition and Feeding* by Sarah Pilliner, though there are many, many great books on the subject.

Forage to Grain Ratio

Most feeds are in fifty-pound bags, so it sounds like your horse would need a half bag of grain per day, right? Wrong. (Very, *very* wrong!) Twenty-five pounds is the *total* ration, including hay, grass, grain, and succulents. Yep, even the carrots and apples we add to the bucket of feed can be included in the amount. For simplicity, let's refer to what the horse is fed as "forage," covering hay (regardless of type) and grazing, and "grain." In the "old days," (and since I remember feeding this way, I guess that makes me old!), we often fed what we called "straights." That is, straight oats/barley/maize etc. This allowed for small, precise alterations to feeding, but there could be wide variations in the quality and nutritional content of these straight grains, as farmers did not carry out testing of every field they harvested. With the advent of modern processed feeds, however, whether pellets or coarse mixes/textured feeds, we now have a much greater assurance of quality and consistent nutritional content. The feed companies have done all of the hard work for us. I think the processed feeds are also more stable and don't tend to go bad as easily as the old-fashioned grains.

The ratio of forage to grain varies depending on a number of factors, from the horse's workload to their temperament and whether they are a hard or easy keeper. (A hard keeper would be a horse whose weight/condition is difficult to maintain and who requires generous amounts of food, while an easy keeper would be one of those who keeps fat and healthy on little more than grass.) As a good rule of thumb, the vast majority of the ration should be forage. These days the general thinking seems to be that the grain portion should be viewed as basically a supplement to good quality forage. Again, the subject of feeding is well covered in many other books, so all I'll do here is a rough overview/example.

Let's assume that this hypothetical 1,000-pound horse is in light work, so ridden maybe two to three times per week for about an hour of walk, trot, and a bit of canter. Maybe the occasional jump. Always remember that feeding regimes should be fluid and that you should make changes only when necessary. (I really think there should be one more "golden rule of feeding," right up there with "make changes gradually." Feeding plans should *never* be set in stone. If it isn't working, *fix it!* But I'm wandering again. Back to our "light work" 1,000-pound horse.) The feed ratio should be around 75:25 or 70:30. We'll work on 75:25 (because the math is simpler). So, that's 75 percent forage, 25 percent grain, or 18¾ pounds forage, 6¼ pounds grain per day. If your horse has access to decent pasture, they will generally be grazing about 1 to 1½ pounds of grass per hour, so if they are turned out all of the time (and allowing that even the greediest horse will sleep *some-times*), their forage intake is pretty well taken care of.

My own horses are turned out for about twelve hours per day (I like them tucked up in their stalls at night) and they don't generally need extra hay to maintain their condition and overall good health. I also give them soaked alfalfa cubes as part of their evening feeds, so they get the extra forage from that as well as fluids (plus, any supplements or medications they need to take will conveniently stick to/dissolve into the soggy alfalfa). If you do need to give additional hay, using a small hanging scale (like those for luggage or fishing) will let you give a feel for the weight of each flake/slice of hay. In general, our bales run about four to five pounds per flake, but if your bales split into very large or very small flakes, you need to again make sure you're feeding by weight. One skimpy two-pound flake is obviously not equal to a "normal" five-pound flake or a giant eight-pound flake! If you're giving hay and finding a lot of it trampled into the ground, cut back what you're giving. Not only is it wasteful (and costly) but as the hay gets wet and starts to rot, it can get *very* slippery.

Grain should be split into at least two feedings per day, usually breakfast and dinner, and at just over three pounds per feed you're looking at probably about one standard-sized scoop per feed, but always check the weight of your particular grain when formulating your feed plan. As an aside, when you are working out your feed plan, remember to take into account your own daily routine. There's no point in working out a nice three-grain-feeds-per-day schedule if you're going to be gone at work in the middle of the day. Most people are home in the morning and evening, so two feeds per day is usually simple to fit into your day.

Once you have the feed amounts sorted out, you can tweak things to get it just right for your horse. If they're getting fat, cut back (despite what many owners seem to think, a fat horse is *not* a healthy horse, any more than being overweight is healthy for humans). Like people, many horses will happily overeat, so just because they're looking for more grain/hay doesn't mean they *need* it! If they drop weight, increase the ration, preferably the forage element. In winter, the most natural way to help your horse stay warm is with lots of forage (hot "mash" feeds really only make the owner feel better). The tough, stemmy part of forage is made of stuff called lignin, and this is broken down and digested in the hind gut by bacteria. As these bacteria do their thing, they give off heat, literally warming the horse from the inside.

I find it useful to take regular (monthly) photos of the horses, because gradual changes in condition are hard to notice when you see them every single day, but comparing photos from a few weeks apart can really show differences, and with smart phones/digital cameras it's easy to take and compare photos. Try to always take roughly the same photo for easiest comparison.

I'm going to leave feeding there. As I said, there are many great books on the science and art of feeding that detail the ins and outs. There are, however, a few long-standing "golden rules" which should always be followed, and these are:

- **Make dietary changes gradually:** Rule of thumb for switching to a new feeding regime is that it should be done over a week to ten days. Start by adding a handful of the new grain per feed (while taking away a handful of the old), then slowly change the ratio of old to new, i.e. three-quarters old, one quarter new; two-thirds old, one-third new; half-and-half; one-third old, two-thirds new; one-quarter old, three-quarters new; all new. Doing this allows the gut flora (all those helpful little "good bugs") to change to most effectively digest the new stuff.

- **Water before feeding:** This stems from the olden days when horses spent their nights in stalls without access to water, and a groom's first priority in the morning was to lead the horses out to water before they were fed. Generally, these days horses will have constant access to water, but it only takes a moment or two to check their bucket and refill, if necessary, before feeding.

- **Increase work before grain; decrease grain before work:** As you work your horse more, whether more frequently or more strenuously, their calorie requirements increase. You should always increase work *then* increase grain, so that your horse doesn't get too "hot" and difficult to ride or handle. In exactly the opposite way, you should decrease their grain *before* decreasing their workload.

- **Try to allow at least an hour between feeding and working your horse:** Some people disagree with the need for this, and I'm sure a great many horses are ridden sooner with no ill effects. I was taught that this break between feeding and riding was to prevent the blood flow being diverted from stomach/digestion to muscles, as this could negatively impact digestion. I really don't know if there is much proven science on this theory, but I've always preferred to play it safe. Anyway, if you let your horse finish eating, by the time you've groomed and tacked up there has been a short delay. And, yes, in the wild, horses may be eating and then suddenly galloping away from a predator, *but* always bear in mind that horses in the wild aren't eating buckets of grain. A short delay in your riding plans is definitely preferable to a vet bill for a colicky horse. Often, though, the easiest thing is just to hold off feeding until after you've ridden.

Okay, now I will *really* leave the subject of feeding.

Feed Charts

A last thing to consider is making out a feed chart. It doesn't have to be anything fancy, just a quick notation of who gets fed what, how much, and when. In case you are sick or otherwise unable to get out to feed your horse, this makes life much easier when you ask someone to help you out. And if you are ill, the last thing you want to do is try to explain about feeds, so jot it down on a piece of paper and put it on the feed room wall. Quick, easy, and super helpful.

Right. This time I'm done!

5

Basic Anatomy and Systems
of the Horse

BASIC anatomy or the so-called "points" of the horse is actually pretty important to know. If you have to call the vet to say your horse has a problem, it's
far more valuable if you can tell them *where* the injury is. Telling them "the
knobby bit on his back leg" is far less useful than saying "his hock" (anyway,
have you noticed how many "knobby" parts there are on a horse's leg?!).

Points of the Horse

Match the numbered points below to their corresponding numbers in the
photo on the next page.

1. Muzzle
2. Nostril
3. Mouth
4. Facial ridge
5. Forehead
6. Forelock
7. Jaw
8. Eye
9. Poll
10. Ear
11. Throat
12. Jugular groove
13. Crest
14. Mane
15. Neck
16. Withers
17. Back
18. Loins
19. Croup
20. Dock/tail head
21. Hip
22. Buttock
23. Barrel/flank
24. Shoulder
25. Point of shoulder
26. Chest
27. Elbow
28. Belly
29. Stifle/patella
30. Tail
31. Forearm
32. Knee
33. Gaskin/thigh
34. Point of hock
35. Hock joint
36. Cannon/splint
    bones
37. Fetlock joint
38. Pastern joint
39. Coronet/coronary
    band
40. Hoof

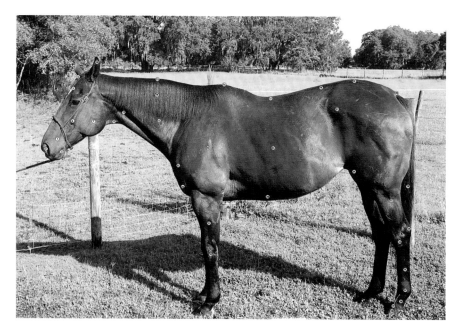

I tried to make my mare stand while I stuck labels all over her, but she declined that suggestion in favor of going out to the field, so this was the best I could do!

Skeletal System

The equine skeletal system can be divided into two distinct sections: the axial skeleton and the appendicular skeleton. The axial skeleton is comprised of the skull, spine, and ribcage. The appendicular skeleton is the limbs.

Axial Skeleton

Cranium (skull): This is made up of a number of smaller bones which are fused together, including the mandible (lower jaw), and atlas and axis, the first two cervical vertebrae at the base of the cranium which form the poll area.

Spine: The spine can be divided into sections from head to tail as follows: the first seven bones are the cervical vertebrae; followed by the eighteen thoracic vertebrae; six lumbar vertebrae; five sacral vertebrae (these are fused together, providing a secure connection point for the pelvis); then finally there are fifteen to twenty coccygeal vertebrae. The number of coccygeal vertebrae varies depending on the length of the horse's dock (tailbone). The purpose of the spine is to provide a secure, protected channel through which the spinal cord can pass from the brain to the end of the body.

Ribcage: The final part of the axial skeleton, the ribcage is formed of eight pairs of "true" ribs, ten pairs of "false" ribs and the sternum (breastbone). The true ribs are attached directly to both spine and sternum, while the false ribs are attached directly to the spine, but are linked to the sternum via long strips of cartilage (the costal cartilages). The ribcage forms a protective cage around the horse's vital organs to shield them from damage.

Appendicular Skeleton

Forelegs: From the top, these are comprised as follows: scapular spine (scapula/shoulder blade); shoulder joint; humerus; elbow joint; radius and ulna (forearm); carpus (knee joint, this is made up of two rows of small bones); accessory carpal/pisiform bone; large metacarpal (cannon bone); small metacarpals (splint bones); fetlock joint; proximal sesamoid; long pastern; pastern joint; short pastern; coffin/pedal joint; navicular bone; pedal (coffin) bone. The accessory carpal, proximal sesamoid, and navicular bones are all "sesamoid" bones, meaning that they are triangular in shape.

Hindlegs: Again, from the top: pelvic girdle/pelvis, made up of three bones (ilium, ischium, and pubis) which are fused together and attached to the spine at the sacral vertebrae; hip joint; femur; patella; stifle joint; tibia and fibula; tarsus (hock joint); os calcis (point of hock); large metatarsal (cannon bone); small metatarsals (splint bones). From this point down the bones are the same as in the forelegs.

Interestingly (or maybe not!) the equine skeleton has a number of similarities to the human skeleton. The forelegs of the horse equate roughly to the human arm and hand, while the hindlegs follow the human leg and foot. This sounds a bit strange, I know, but noted below are the equivalents for information anyway.

Horse	Human
Humerus	Humerus (upper arm)
Elbow joint	Elbow joint

Radius and ulna (forearm)	Radius and ulna (forearm)
Knee (carpus) joint	Wrist (carpus) joint
Cannon bone	Bone to middle finger
Splint bones	Bones to index/fourth fingers
Long pastern	First bone of middle finger
Short pastern	Second bone of middle finger
Pedal bone	Middle fingertip bone
Pelvis	Pelvis
Hip joint	Hip joint
Femur	Femur (thigh bone)
Stifle joint/patella	Knee joint/patella (kneecap)
Tibia and fibula	Tibia and fibula (lower leg)
Hock joint (tarsus)	Ankle joint (tarsus)
Point of hock (os calcis)	Heel bone
Cannon bone	Bone to middle toe
Splint bones	Bones to first/fourth toes
Long pastern	First bone of middle toe
Short pastern	Second bone of middle toe
Pedal bone	Bone at tip of middle toe

Obviously both horses and humans also have skulls, jaws, ribcages, and spines. In fact, one of the only bones which they don't share is the clavicle—horses don't have them!

Digestive System

Anatomy

The digestive system runs from mouth to anus. The first stage of the digestive process begins when the horse uses its exceptionally mobile lips (particularly the upper lip) to select food (grass, for example). The lips of the horse are sensitive to taste, which enables them to easily avoid poisonous plants or those which are unpalatable. In the same way, a horse can avoid any part of their feed which they do not find pleasing, such as medications or dewormer granules, which is why these must be mixed thoroughly into the feed (and preferably mixed with beet pulp or molasses to make it more difficult for the horse to avoid!).

Once a mouthful of food has been selected, the horse will bite it off with the incisor (front) teeth and use the tongue to push the food back to the molars for grinding down into small enough pieces for easy swallowing. On average, this will take an amazing 1,600–2,500 chews per pound of grain or 6,000–7,000 chews per pound of hay!

During chewing, the ingested food is mixed with saliva (of which a horse produces around three to three and a half gallons per day) which has little or no digestive value, but lubricates the passage of the ingesta through the esophagus. Saliva also contains bicarbonate, whose alkaline properties help to buffer the acid produced in the stomach. Salivary production is stimulated by the action of chewing, and there are three pairs of salivary glands: parotid, mandibular, and sublingual.

The ingesta is now swallowed, passing through the pharynx into the esophagus. As the food passes through the pharynx, this triggers the epiglottis to close off the trachea, preventing the food "going down the wrong way" and entering the lungs. The esophagus itself is simply a tube, four to five feet long, which carries the ingesta down to the stomach. No digestion takes place within the esophagus.

Stomach: The horse's stomach is relatively small for the size of the animal, around the size of a football, and is roughly J-shaped. The entry of ingesta to the stomach is controlled by a strong sphincter (ring) muscle called the cardiac sphincter. This sphincter muscle is a one-way valve, which is the reason why horses are physically unable to vomit.

The stomach can be roughly divided into four regions: esophageal, cardiac, fundic, and pyloric. The stomach is designed to work best when it is two-thirds full, and this combined with the size of the stomach explains one of the golden rules of feeding: feed little and often. If the horse is given too much at one time, food will be pushed through the stomach too quickly, before the digestive juices have properly treated the food, and the horse will not receive full nutritional benefit.

The first of the four regions of the stomach is the esophageal, which contains no digestive glands and is mainly a storage area. Next is the cardiac region (so called as it lies nearest the heart) where mucus is added to the ingesta. The mucus has no digestive value, but protects the stomach lining against the digestive juices. The third region of the stomach is the largest, and this is the fundic region. Here hydrochloric acid is added to the ingesta, which must remain in the stomach until the acid is sufficiently absorbed. Within the fundic region, enzymes* for digestion of food are also secreted, along with mucus. The ingesta moves through to the final region, the pyloric, where more mucus and enzymes are produced by the pyloric glands. Ingesta now exits the stomach through another sphincter muscle, the pyloric sphincter. On leaving the stomach, the ingesta is very acidic and therefore would damage the small intestine if not neutralized. About six inches from the pyloric sphincter, the bile duct enters the digestive tract and bile is added to the ingesta, which is now known as chyme. The horse does not have a gallbladder in which to store bile, so there is a steady flow of bile into the digestive tract, which is linked to the fact that the horse is a trickle feeder with a digestive system designed to have food constantly traveling through.

Small intestine: After exiting the stomach (where food generally spends less than an hour) food passes into the small intestine, a tube which runs from the stomach to the large intestine. The small intestine is where the majority of the concentrate (grain) portion of the horse's diet is processed. The total length of the small intestine is around sixty-five to eighty-eight feet, with a capacity of twelve to sixteen gallons. The small intestine is composed of three parts: the duodenum, jejunum, and ileum. The duodenum is comprised of the first three feet or so of the small intestine, and is closely attached to the stomach. The duodenum forms an S-shaped curve which contains the pancreas. The pancreatic and bile ducts enter the duodenum around six inches from the pyloric sphincter. The next sixty-five or so feet lead you to the jejunum, followed by the ileum, the final three to five feet of the small intestine. The jejunum and ileum lie to the left side of the horse, between the stomach and pelvis. Other than its attachments to the stomach and caecum, the small intestine lies in numerous coils along with the small colon, and is able to move quite freely within the abdominal space.

---

*Enzymes are catalysts, substances which promote a chemical reaction without themselves being changed by the reaction. Every living cell within the body contains catalysts or enzymes which enable the cell to carry out the complex chemical reactions necessary to sustain life.

The small intestine contains three types of glands which produce many digestive enzymes. Duodenal (Brunner's) glands are found in the first area of the small intestine (the duodenum), while intestinal glands (crypts of Lieberkuhn) and Peyer's patches are found throughout the length of the small intestine.

Large intestine: So far, the process of digestion in the horse is very similar to that found in human beings, yet the horse can stay fit and healthy on grass and other vegetation. Humans, on the other hand, do not necessarily thrive on this diet. So, where is the difference? The answer lies in the specially evolved hind gut (large intestine) of the horse where the energy stored within the tough, fibrous parts of plants is released. The horse does not possess digestive enzymes which can break down the complex insoluble carbohydrates that form the cell walls of plant material. However, this can be accomplished through fermentation, and the horse's hind gut *does* contain a vast number of microorganisms (bacteria) that are perfectly happy to ferment their way through the cellulose, hemicellulose, and pectin to get to the energy locked within. The large intestine extends about twenty-five feet from the ileum to the anus and consists of four parts:

- **Caecum:** A large blind-ended, comma-shaped sac, the caecum sits at the end of the small intestine. The entrance lies close to the horse's right hip bone, running forward and down for two to three feet, ending midway along the horse's belly, lying on the abdominal floor. The caecum has a capacity of six to eight gallons.
- **Large colon:** With a capacity of twenty to twenty-five gallons and a length of ten to fourteen feet, the large colon must fold into four regions just to fit into the horse's abdomen. These four regions, starting from the caecum, are known as the right ventral colon, left ventral colon, left dorsal colon, and right dorsal colon, with defined bends (flexures) between each region. The large colon narrows after the sternal flexure (the bend between right and left ventral sections), then narrows even further, to as little as two and a half inches, around the pelvic flexure before expanding rapidly as it approaches the diaphragm to the left

dorsal colon. The final turn, the diaphragmatic flexure, leads on to the right dorsal colon, which narrows as it merges with the small colon. The large colon is held in place by only its bulk, and if the gut is not kept sufficiently full (i.e. with an adequate amount of forage in the diet), this can lead to problems. Those areas where the colon narrows and changes direction are vulnerable to blockages, which could cause colic. Most of what the horse eats will reach the caecum three hours after a meal and will then spend thirty-six to forty-eight hours transiting the large intestine.

- **Small colon:** This is around ten to thirteen feet in length, but narrower than the large colon, with a capacity of only two to sixteen gallons. The small colon lies within the same space as the jejunum and is able to move quite freely, which can lead to twisted gut in some cases of colic.

- **Rectum:** The final part of the digestive tract is the rectum which connects the small colon to the anus, serving as a storage area for feces.

Digestive Process

Now that we have at least a basic understanding of the structure of the horse's digestive system, let's take a quick run through "what happens where." First, food is moved through the entirety of the digestive tract by involuntary muscle movements known as peristalsis.

Stomach

Not much actual digestion happens in the stomach. Rather, this is an area where food is made ready for digestion. Food entering the stomach activates the fundic glands to produce gastric juices which contain enzymes—pepsin and gastric lipase—and hydrochloric acid. Pepsin is an enzyme which digests protein to so-called intermediate products: proteoses and peptones; it is secreted as pepsinogen and activated to pepsin by the accompanying acid. Gastric lipase has only a minimal role here, helping to reduce fat to fatty acids and glycerol. Hydrochloric acid is actually one of the most vital components of the gastric juice as this is what activates pepsin, and also serves as an antiseptic for the stomach, killing any bacteria which may have been ingested. Due to the alkaline nature of saliva, production of which is stimulated by chewing, the different stomach regions have markedly different levels of acidity, with the contents progressing from an alkaline state to a highly acidic state as they move through the stomach.

Small Intestine

The ingesta is highly acidic upon leaving the stomach, but the digestive process in the small intestine requires alkaline conditions, so to transform the pH of the ingesta, pancreatic juice and bile from the liver enter the small intestine. Bile not only neutralizes the acid, but it also emulsifies fats, increasing their surface area to encourage more efficient use of fat-digesting lipase enzymes. Unlike humans, the horse has no gallbladder, so bile continuously trickles into the small intestine. The digestive process makes use of a great number of digestive enzymes, those catalysts which break down foods into simple substances which can be absorbed by the body for its various requirements. I will not list them all, but just define the three types: proteases (protein-digesting enzymes), amylases (carbohydrate-digesting enzymes), and lipases (fat-digesting enzymes).

So, what do these groups of enzymes do?

- **Proteases:** Unlike the stomach, the small intestine performs a substantial amount of protein digestion, with the proteins being finally broken down to amino acids, the simple building blocks of life. These amino acids, predominantly those extracted from the grain portion of the diet, are absorbed through the gut wall and into the bloodstream.
- **Amylases:** Water-soluble carbohydrates, sugars and cereal starches, are also broken down in the small intestine. Horses are evolved to eat grasses, which have a much lower starch content than the concentrated feeds used with most domestic horses, and this can cause problems if the complex starches cannot be broken down during the comparatively short time the starch is in the small intestine. The digestion of starch is difficult since starch is chemically complex, consisting of many bonded glucose molecules. This is another reason to

ensure your horse receives more forage than grain in their feed ration.

- **Lipases:** These enzymes hydrolyze fat, previously emulsified by bile, into fatty acids and glycerol. These resultant products are absorbed across the intestinal wall to the lymphatic system, which then transport tiny fat droplets to the bloodstream.

Food moves fairly quickly through the small intestine, with food particles passing into the caecum in just over an hour. Nonfibrous/soluble feeds will already have been substantially digested by this time through the action of these various enzymes.

Large Intestine

Water is absorbed throughout the length of the large intestine so that by the time the digesta reaches the rectum it is of a firm consistency. The caecum and large colon serve mainly as an environment where millions of microorganisms can ferment insoluble carbohydrates to release acetic, propionic, and butyric acids, or volatile fatty acids (VFA). These VFA are absorbed into the bloodstream to provide the horse with a source of energy. It is this mechanism which allows horses to thrive on their natural diet of forage. The horse's gut holds ten times more bacteria than there are cells in the body, and more than half of the manure produced is actually bacteria!

The huge number of bacteria within the gut are of various types, each dependent upon diet. The specialization of bacteria is the primary reason for another rule of feeding: make changes gradually. Slowly transitioning to new feed allows the bacterial population to adjust, thus ensuring that the efficiency of the horse's digestive process is not compromised.

Another useful aspect of this bacterial population is that a by-product of fermentation is heat, so by ensuring your horse has adequate forage in winter, those helpful little bugs will keep your horse warm from the inside.

Respiratory and Circulatory Systems

Respiratory System

Oxygen, present with other gases in the air, is a fuel essential to mammals. Deprived of oxygen, the body begins to deteriorate quickly. A horse would only survive for a matter of minutes without oxygen, as brain cells begin to die rapidly and muscles stop working, which is serious for vital organs such as the heart. To maintain life, air is inhaled, and oxygen is extracted and distributed around the body. This is the prime function of the respiratory system.

The functions of the respiratory system are:

1. Take in oxygen
2. Remove waste products: water and carbon dioxide
3. Regulate body temperature
4. Create sound
5. Act as a sensory organ

Upper Respiratory Tract

Air is taken in first through the nostrils, not the mouth. The nostrils change shape when the horse inhales. During hard work, for example, the nostrils expand to inhale more air. Horses are not able to breathe through their mouths. Lining the nostrils are small *cilia* hairs which act as filters, trapping dust and other foreign particles entering the system. Continuing on from the nostrils are two nasal passages (one for each nostril). These are separated by a partition made of bone and cartilage, the *septum*. Dividing the nasal passages from the mouth is the palate. Toward the mouth the palate is hard, but nearer the throat the palate becomes a soft, muscular membrane. Behind the nasal passages is the *pharynx*, a single cavity divided horizontally by the soft palate. The top portion is the *nasopharynx* and the lower the *oropharynx* at the back of the mouth. There are other air-filled cavities in this area: the *sinuses* and the *guttural pouches*. Both the gullet and the trachea start at the pharynx. The trachea is a tube kept permanently open by rings of cartilage. The larynx, or voice box, is situated at the top of the trachea. This is a tube of cartilage plates held together by membranes and muscle fibers, all covered by a mucus lining.

The larynx has three main functions:

1. **Acting as a valve, regulating the air flow:** When the horse is resting, the respiration is relatively shallow, but as the horse needs more air, for instance during exercise, the larynx widens.

During hard, fast work, the larynx is fully opened to allow a maximum amount of air into the respiratory system.

2. **Protecting of the respiratory system:** Prevents food or foreign particles entering the respiratory system. The trachea in the neck lies below (or in front of) the gullet. The food being swallowed from the mouth has to cross over the top of the trachea into the esophagus. To prevent food or other particles from entering the respiratory system, a coordinated action by the *epiglottis* and larynx effectively blocks off the top of the trachea. The epiglottis is a flat of cartilage at the top of the larynx. When the horse swallows, the soft palate moves upward to the roof of the mouth, cutting off the nasal passages. The epiglottis closes over the larynx. The larynx itself moves upward and forward toward the epiglottis, shutting off the trachea and allowing the gullet to open. When air is inhaled, the soft palate at the back of the throat is lowered and the epiglottis slightly overlaps it. Air is taken in and passes through the larynx into the trachea. In humans, the movement of the larynx can be seen when the "Adam's apple" moves up and down. This takes place within a few seconds.

3. **Producing sound:** Some of the fibers within the larynx act as vocal cords, creating sound when air is exhaled. When the horse breathes in, the air passes through the larynx into the windpipe or trachea. The trachea, which can be felt quite easily down the underside of the horse's neck, is also lined with cilia that filter the air passing into the lungs.

Lower Respiratory Tract

The lungs are two large elastic organs taking up most of the chest cavity, apart from the space occupied by the heart, major blood vessels, esophagus, lymph tubes, and glands. In the chest, the trachea splits into two branches, called *bronchi*. These tubes are kept permanently open by rings of cartilage. One branch goes to each lung, where they divide again into narrower branches called *bronchioles*. These are not supported by cartilage. The bronchioles divide into tiny ducts called *alveoli* which, in turn, terminate as air sacs. The alveolar sacs have the appearance of bunches of grapes. These thin-walled sacs are covered with narrow blood vessels, the *capillaries*. This design gives a much larger surface area for the exchange of gases. All the airways within the respiratory system contain tiny, hair-like cilia. On top of the cilia is a tiny film of mucus. Dust and other foreign particles collected in this mucus are carried by the cilia in a wave-like motion through the airways to the throat. The horse then swallows the mucus. Situated behind the lungs and assisting with respiration is a sheet of muscle called the *diaphragm*. This stretches from the loins under the spine, sloping downward and forward to the sternum. It is cone or dome shaped when relaxed, like an open umbrella. The main artery of the body, the *aorta*, the main vein, the *vena cava*, and the esophagus pass through it.

Respiration

At rest the horse takes eight to sixteen breaths per minute. The respiration rate increases at certain times, e.g. after work or when stressed, nervous, or ill. After exercise, the rate can increase up to 120 breaths per minute. The act of breathing starts within the respiratory center of the brain. This controls breathing so that no conscious effort need be made, though the rapidity or depth of breathing can, to some degree, be consciously controlled. The *intercostal muscles*, between the ribs, together with the diaphragm, contract. This has the effect of bringing the ribs outward and expanding the size of the lungs. The increased chest cavity creates a lower air pressure in the lungs than in the atmosphere, and air is drawn into the lungs. When the muscles relax, the chest cavity reduces in size and air is exhaled. The chest cavity and lungs are covered with a smooth, moist membrane called the *pleura*. This allows the lungs to slide smoothly against each other and within the chest, preventing friction during expansion and contraction. Air is sucked in and travels through the airways to the alveolar sacs. The blood vessels (capillaries) that cover the sacs have extremely thin walls, so the oxygen is able to pass (diffuse) into the bloodstream. Carbon dioxide and water vapor diffuse from the bloodstream into the alveoli and are excreted through the nostrils. The water vapor acts to keep the air in the respiratory tubes moist. When the horse is resting, only a percentage of the lung capacity is used. The harder the horse works, the more oxygen is needed for muscle activity. The respiratory rate increases and breathing becomes deeper. More of the lung capacity, that is a greater number of alveoli, is put into use to pass this oxygen into the bloodstream.

Heat Regulation

When the body is hot and needs to lose heat, one method is through respiration. Breathing is increased in speed and depth so cool air is inhaled. This cools the blood in the capillaries of the lungs. Warm air is exhaled and heat is lost from the body. During cold weather, air is warmed up slightly as it enters the body to prevent the chill air from striking the lungs. The air being exhaled is warmer and visible as steam.

Sound Production

The horse can give a variety of sounds, from a soft whinny to a bellow or a squeal, using the vocal cords within the larynx. Air is exhaled and fibers in the larynx vibrate to produce the desired sounds.

Sense of Smell

In the nasal passages there are delicate bones (*turbinates*). The mucus membranes covering these bones have a rich blood supply and contain the nerve cells concerned with smell (*olfactory*). From the membranes, tiny hairs (*sensory cilia*) grow. As the air passes over and touches the membranes, it stimulates the cilia. The cilia pass the message onto the nerve cells and then, through nervous impulses, to the brain. The nostrils can indicate the horse's emotions by contracting tightly, blowing out, or strong sniffing.

External and Internal Respiration

External respiration: The inhalation of oxygen to the lungs and the eventual exhalation of waste products: carbon dioxide and water.

Internal respiration: The exchange of oxygen for carbon dioxide through the body. Oxygen is vital for the functioning of the body tissues and is needed to excrete a horse's waste products.

Muscles, Tendons, and Ligaments

Muscle Composition

Skeletal muscle is composed of millions of long, slender fibers otherwise known as *myofibrils*. Each fiber is a single cell, elongated and cylindrical in shape. These fibers lie parallel to each other, supported and bound by connective tissue. This connective tissue binds the muscle fibers to the tendons at either end. When stimulated by a nervous impulse, the myofibrils slide over one another, causing the muscle to shorten, thicken, and therefore contract. The muscle fibers themselves do not actually shorten. These muscle fibers are found in the muscle belly which has a tendon at either end. Muscle bellies come in various shapes and sizes, some are flat and sheet-like, as are the latissimus dorsi, external abdominal oblique, and trapezius. The muscle fibers in these cases are long, offering a wide range of movement, with flattened tendinous attachments. Long, strap-like muscles such as the brachiocephalic also have long fibers. The muscles of the forearm and thigh have shorter fibers, densely packed in the belly, resulting in greater strength. These are known as *pennate muscles.* The contraction of muscles requires a supply of energy. Tiny cells called *mitochondria* generate this energy. Muscle cells contain the carbohydrate energy-giving substance, glycogen, which is broken down to release this energy through a chemical reaction caused by enzymes also stored in the muscle cells. Oxygen is brought to the muscles through the blood supply and is stored in the red muscle pigment, *myoglobin*, a protein which can bind oxygen to itself. Free fatty acids are present in the blood or stored in the muscles. Energy is released when these are broken down by enzymes Waste products such as carbon dioxide are created as a result of muscular activity. These waste products are removed via the bloodstream.

Muscle Fibers

Red muscle fibers known as *actin* contain a large amount of myoglobin, enabling the use of larger amounts of oxygen. This is high-oxidative muscle. White muscle fibers, known as *myosin* have a lower capacity for using oxygen and are known as low-oxidative muscle. Slow-twitch muscles are those which have slower contractions but a greater capacity for using oxygen. It is these muscles that are important in any endurance work. Fast-twitch muscles contract quickly and are either high oxidative, which enable a horse to work at speed over distances, or low oxidative, which are used for acceleration, but result in the horse tiring easily. All muscles contain these three types of fiber: slow-twitch, high-oxidative fast-twitch, and low-oxidative fast-twitch. The muscle responds according to the work being done.

Tendons

A tendon is a fibrous cord of connective tissue continuous with the fibers of a muscle, attaching the muscle to bone, cartilage, or other muscle. Tendons form in the embryo from fibroblasts, which proliferate, becoming tightly packed, thus allowing the tendons to grow. As development continues, they become arranged in longitudinal rows and secrete collagen, the main supporting protein of connective tissue. Collagen lies between the rows of fibroblasts, forming an intercellular substance. While developing, the cells require a good blood and nutrient supply. Once development is complete, this supply disappears, making repair of injured or severed tendons difficult. Tendons insert into bone or cartilage by means of small spicules known as "Sharpey's Fibers." When a muscle needs a wide area of attachment, the tendon spreads out to form an *aponeurosis.*

Tendon Sheath

When a tendon is in a position to rub against bone or other hard surfaces, it is enclosed in a sheath. This takes the form of an inner sheath which encloses and is firmly attached to the tendon, and an outer connective tissue tube which is attached to its surrounding surface. The space between the two sheaths is filled with a lubricant similar to synovial fluid.

Ligaments

Ligaments are composed of bands of white and yellow fibrous tissue, the white being inelastic and the yellow elastic. They are somewhat flexible, while their consistency is tough and unyielding. Ligaments are poorly supplied with blood but are rich in sensory nerves. Due to the poor blood supply, they are very slow to heal. Ligaments do not withstand prolonged stretching. If a joint is forced beyond its limitations as set by the ligament, a sprain will occur. Ligamentous injury is extremely painful. Due to the fact that the ligaments and muscles are usually stronger than the bone to which they are attached, any severe stress is more likely to break the bone than dislocate the joint or tear the ligament.

Ligaments and their functions:

1. Suspensory: supporting or suspending

2. Annular: broad bands composed of deep fascia which holds tendons down
3. Interosseous: ties bones together, e.g. pedal and navicular
4. Funicular or cordlike: holds bones together

Ligaments help to limit the movement of joints accordingly; for example, the fetlock, pastern, and coffin joints have *collateral ligaments* on their inner and outer aspects to confine movement to a forward and backward movement only. Ligaments attach to the bone through blending with the periosteum. They allow a certain amount of movement; the more movement that is required, the more yellow elastic tissue would be present in that ligament. The ligaments holding an immovable joint together will comprise all inelastic white tissue.

Major Ligaments

The muscle groups around the spine are designed to support the spine in conjunction with the abdominal muscles and important ligaments below. These ligaments are attached to the vertebrae along the length of the spine and are the:

- **Ventral ligament:** lies on the underside of vertebrae.
- **Dorsal ligament:** forms the floor of the spinal canal.
- **Supraspinous ligament:** attaches at the poll and extends down to the sacrum. In the withers and neck area, fan-like extensions reach down and attach to the spines of the cervical vertebrae. This area known as the nuchal ligament helps to support the head and neck while maintaining a traction force to the spine which assists in supporting the spine, particularly in the potentially weak thoracolumbar area.
- **Sacrosciatic ligament:** extends from the sacrum and coccygeal vertebrae down to the pelvic bone below, forming the basis of the pelvic walls. This ligament is in the form of a sheet which fuses with part of the hamstring group.
- **Suspensory ligament:** lies between the two splint bones close to the back of the cannon bone, originating close to the knee. It descends toward the fetlock joint, above which it divides into

two branches. Each branch attaches to the corresponding sesa-moid bone while some fibers blend in with the common digital extensor tendon. The suspensory ligament provides a form of support for the fetlock joint, preventing it from extending down-ward too far toward the ground which would increase the risk of strains.

- **Check ligament:** lies below the knee and prevents undue strain being applied to the flexor tendons; it also assists in supporting the horse, thus allowing them to sleep whilst standing. This ligament is connected to the deep flexor tendon. There is also a check ligament above the knee which connects to the superficial flexor tendon. The superficial and deep flexor tendons extend down from their muscles in the forearm through to the foot, acting as main weight bearers, assisted by the check ligaments.

Joints

Joints occur where two or more bones meet each other. Their type and form are determined by the function and degree of mobility required. Not all joints are constructed to allow movement, nor are they necessarily permanent.

Joints are divided into four main groups:

- Bony
- Fibrous
- Cartilaginous
- Synovial

Bony joints: the three elements of the hip—the ileum, ischium, and pubis.

Fibrous joints: fixed joints composed of fibrous connective tissue between bones, e.g. skull sutures.

Cartilaginous joints: divided into primary and secondary cartilaginous joints. Primary joints are where bony surfaces are united by cartilage as seen in the epiphyseal plates in long bones before ossification. Secondary cartilaginous joints are united by a fibrocartilaginous disc as in the intervertebral discs.

This joint provides a resilient bond as is needed in the spine; the movement passable is dependent on the thickness of the disc.

Synovial joints: free-moving joints, the bones of which are linked by a fibrous capsule. The bone ends are covered by cartilage which, aided by synovial fluid, reduces friction. This synovial fluid is secreted by the synovial membrane which lines the joint capsule. Articular cartilage is able to withstand great forces of compression due to its wear-resistant, low-friction, slightly compressible, and elastic surface. Although smooth in appearance it is, in fact, a series of valleys and peaks with synovial fluid being trapped in the valleys. It has a porous nature, resembling a sponge. As it is closely molded to bone, it has no nutrient blood vessels, therefore it receives nutrition from the vascular network in the synovial membrane and blood vessels in the marrow cavities. Young cartilage is white and glistening but, with age, it becomes thinner, firmer, and more brittle with a less regular surface and a yellow color. There is less synovial fluid, therefore more friction occurs.

Synovial Membrane

This membrane lines the nonarticular part of a synovial joint and all tendon sheaths. Its surface is lubricated by an egg white–like fluid, *synovia*, which is secreted and absorbed by the membrane. Synovial fluid is a clear, pale yellow, viscous, slightly alkaline fluid, containing a mixed population of cells. Its functions are to provide a liquid environment and nutritive source for the articular cartilage and discs. It also acts as a lubricant and helps to reduce the erosion of joint surfaces.

Classification of Synovial Joints

If a joint has two articular surfaces it is known as a simple joint. If more, it is known as a compound joint.

Hinge joint: allows a to-and-fro movement, convex to concave surface, e.g. pastern joint

Plane joint: fairly flat articular surfaces which give a gliding movement, such as is found between the articular processes of adjacent vertebrae

Pivot joint: a peg-like process rotates in a socket allowing a sideways head turning, e.g. joint between the atlas and axis

Condylar joint: a knuckle-shaped surface articulates with a deep, cup-shaped cavity, e.g. the joint between the atlas and occipital bone (skull); allows movement in a single place, i.e. head nodding up and down

Ball-and-socket joint: globular head of one bone fits into cup-like cavity (acetabulum) of another, e.g. hip joint

Structure of the Foot

The foot is one of the most important parts of the horse. The old saying "no foot, no horse" is very true. When you consider that an average of 1,000 pounds is ultimately resting on four points which can each be covered with a spread hand, it makes sense that any problems in this area may be very serious. But the feet are not only vital parts of the horse's physical support structure, they also assist with correct performance of the circulatory system.

The structures of the foot may be divided broadly into three sections: the skeletal, sensitive, and insensitive. Roughly speaking, the sensitive and insensitive correspond to the parts we can actually see. The skeletal part is also obviously not visible, and is comprised of the bones and cartilages of the foot. Another vital component is the digital or plantar cushion.

The foot contains three bones: the third or distal* phalanx, commonly called the pedal or coffin bone; the second phalanx, the short pastern bone; the navicular bone. The pedal bone is roughly the same shape as the visible hoof and lies toward the front of the foot, parallel to the outer hoof wall. The short pastern lies above the pedal bone, and the navicular bone, a small sesamoid-type bone, is situated behind the pedal bone and below the short pastern. The navicular bone is attached to both of the other bones of the foot by the distal and suspensory navicular ligaments (distal connects to the pedal bone while the suspensory attaches to the short pastern).

---

*Distal denotes that this bone is farthest from the body, while proximal would mean the bone closest to the body.

The *deep digital flexor tendon* runs behind all of these to attach to the underside of the pedal bone. This tendon is closely associated with two major conditions which may occur in the foot: laminitis/founder and navicular disease. The joint between the pedal and short pastern bones is called the coffin joint, and this lies almost exactly behind the coronary band, which is the visible intersection of the hoof wall and the skin of the leg.

The *accessory cartilages* (also known as the lateral cartilages) are flexible structures extending from the sides of the pedal bone. These cartilages reach out toward the back of the foot and wrap around the sides of the plantar cushion, acting as a shock absorber within the hoof capsule, and also playing an important role in the horse's circulatory system.

In the simplest terms, blood flow down the leg is greatly assisted by gravity, but the return flow up through the veins is aided when the horse moves. When the foot is laid down, the *frog*, the V-shaped part in the rear center of the sole, is pressed against the ground and pushes up slightly. Above the frog lies the plantar cushion, hemmed in by the lateral cartilages. As the upward pressure of the frog compresses the cushion, the pressure pushes the cushion against the lateral cartilages which in turn press against the inside of the coronary band, squeezing blood out of structures called venous plexuses and back up the leg. As noted, this is a very simplified explanation of the process, but still probably more than you really wanted to know!

The sensitive foot has three sections. The coronary band lies at the junction between the skin and the hoof wall, and this produces horn cells, effectively growing new hooves in the same way our own nail beds produce new nails. Horn growth occurs at a rate of around ⅜ inch (1 centimeter) per month, so it can take eight to ten months for an entirely new hoof to grow, something to bear in mind if you decide to use a dietary hoof supplement, as you will have to persevere for quite some time before any real benefit is felt.

Between the coronary band and the sole of the foot are the *sensitive laminae*, which are attached to the pedal bone. The sensitive laminae consists of around 600 leaves which, in combination with the interwoven insensitive laminae, serve to support and suspend the pedal bone. In cases of laminitis, these sensitive laminae become inflamed and painful, leading to horses displaying the characteristic laminitic posture as they attempt to keep their weight on their heels to lessen pain. Severe cases, known as founder, cause the bonds between the two sets of laminae to detach, removing the vital pedal bone support and allowing the pedal bone to rotate down to (and sometimes even *through*) the sole. This loss of support is exacerbated by the pull of the deep digital flexor tendon.

The final part of the sensitive foot is the *periople*, which lies above the coronary band and secretes a waterproofing layer of varnish which coats the hoof wall as it grows. This varnish minimizes moisture loss and aids in prevention of hoof shrinkage and splitting. Last, the insensitive foot is comprised of those parts which are clearly visible. The hoof wall is made up of dense horn and on the inside are the *insensitive laminae* which interlock with their sensitive counterparts. At the back of the foot, at the heels, the hoof wall folds inward to form the bars of the foot. The bars help to maintain the shape of the hoof wall and prevent it from contracting.

The *sole* is, obviously, the sole of the foot, which serves as both a shock absorber and more generally just as a protective layer for the sensitive structures within the foot. Soles tend to vary in thickness, and a very thin-soled horse will be more prone to sole bruises. Located between the sole and the hoof wall is the white line, and this marks the intersection of the sensitive and insensitive portions of the foot. This is of great importance to your farrier if he is nailing on shoes, as it clearly defines the thickness of the hoof wall and shows where he may safely drive nails without causing injury. The soles are usually somewhat concave so that the actual weight-bearing surface is the hoof wall and the frog.

Again, the frog is the V-shaped part in the rear center of the sole, situated between the bars, and this acts as a shock absorber as well as improving grip and traction. As previously mentioned, the frog also acts on the plantar cushion. Behind the frog, at the very back of the foot, are the heels. The network of veins just below the skin in this area makes it one of the places where a pulse may be easily felt.

Sight and Hearing

To avoid their natural predators, horses have developed into a species capable of great speed. For this ability to get out of danger quickly, the horse has also had to develop highly sophisticated senses, in this case, sight and hearing.

Sight

The eyes are positioned high on the head and are set more to the side than the front, offering an extremely wide field of vision. In fact, the horse has

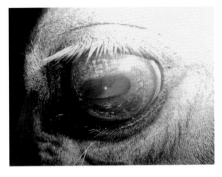

an almost 360-degree field of vision, with only minimal blind spots directly in front and behind and in the areas directly alongside the body. Each eye offers a 146-degree monocular field of vision to the side, while there is a 65-degree field of binocular vision to the front of the horse. Binocular vision allows for depth/ height perception, which is why a horse will lower their head slightly on approach to a jump, to better gauge the height and distance.

On either side of the skull there is a cavity called the *orbit* which is surrounded by bone. The eyes lie within the orbits. Above and in front of the eye, the skull bone is more prominent, forming a rigid arch known as the supraorbital process. This arch is particularly strong, providing protection to the eye.

To the front of the eye are the *nasal bones* and *facial crest* (an easily seen bony ridge on the side of the face, sometimes referred to, incorrectly, as the cheekbone) while below the eye are the jaw muscles. These various structures form a circle around each eye which very effectively protects the eyes against injuries.

Within the orbit itself, a large pad of fat lies behind the eye, acting as a cushion which absorbs and dissipates the force of any direct blow to the eye. These elements, combined with excellent reflexes, mean that eye injuries are thankfully quite rare.

Structure of the Eye

The horse has two external eyelids and one inner eyelid which is located at the front corner of the eye, between the eye and the outer lids. This third eyelid is composed of mucus membrane and cartilage and assists with lubrication of the eye by spreading tears across the surface. The outer eyelids are composed of cartilage with skin covering the outside while the inside is covered by the *conjunctiva*, the moist pink membrane lining the eyelids. The eyelashes mark the point where the skin meets the conjunctiva at the edge of the eyelid. The tear ducts are found in the inner corner of the eye and these merge to form the nasolacrimal duct, running below the nasal bones and associated cartilage to discharge on the floor of each nostril. Actual tears are secreted by the lacrimal gland, which is found beneath the supraorbital process. Should a horse's tear ducts become obstructed, the tears will overflow the lower eyelid and run down the side of the face. Over time, this can cause scalding of the skin and result in hair loss to the affected area. The moist pink membrane lining the eyelids and covering the third eyelid is the conjunctiva. From the inside of the eyelids, this reverses direction to cover the eyeball and forms part of the cornea as the bulbar conjunctiva. The *cornea* is the thick, tough, transparent tissue visible between the eyelids that forms the front portion of the eyeball. This merges into the sclera, the white of the eye. The cornea is shaped like a horizontal egg, with the fat end of the egg positioned toward the front of the face.

The internal components of the eyeball are encapsulated by the wall of the eyeball. This wall is comprised of three layers: sclera, choroid, and retina. The sclera is the outside layer, and at the front of the eye the cornea sits in the sclera. The sclera is made of a tough white tissue, giving strength to the eyeball. When you see the white around a horse's eye when they are scared or nervous, what you are actually seeing is the sclera where it meets the cornea. The sclera is lined by the choroid layer. Extending from the optic nerve to the ciliary body, the thin membrane of the choroid layer lies between the sclera and retina. The retina is the final thin membrane layer, lining the inner surface of the choroid. Light-sensitive, the retina is in contact with the vitreous humor and is formed with an extremely complex network of nerves and blood vessels. The retina receives the images seen by the horse, transmitting them via the optic nerve to the brain.

From front to back, the interior of the eyeball is as follows: cornea; anterior chamber (containing aqueous humor); iris/pupil; posterior chamber; lens; posterior segment (containing vitreous humor); retina. The *iris* is the colored part of the eye and has a gap through its center, called the pupil. A muscular diaphragm, the iris is able to alter the size of the pupil dependent upon light. In bright light, the pupil will contract to limit light ingress. In darker conditions, the pupil can enlarge to maximize use of available light. The edges of the pupil are not uniform but display pigmented projections called corpora nigra. These are larger on the upper edge and can usually be clearly seen, like a fuzzy caterpillar between the colored iris and the pupil. I have heard it suggested that this "caterpillar" acts as a sort of natural sunshade. The *lens* is transparent and circular and is convex to both front and rear, with the front less curved than the rear. Thanks to muscular connections to the eyeball (the ciliary body), the lens can alter its degree of convexity (when the muscles pull, the lens flattens out a little more and vice versa) and this mechanism allows the horse to focus at different distances. At the rear of the eyeball, the optic nerve enters and passes through the sclera and choroid before fanning out filaments which form the retina.

So, how does vision work? Simply put, rays of light enter the eyeball where the cornea and lens angle the beams to converge on the retina. The ability of the lens to change shape allows the horse to focus on objects at different distances, while the pupil controls the amount of light being allowed to enter. The focused light which reaches the retina is then transmitted along the optic nerve to the brain as nervous impulses where they are translated into visual images. As in our own eyes, the "picture" on the retina is actually inverted and has to be turned right-way up by the brain.

Hearing

The ear is made up of three distinct parts: the outer ear, middle ear, and inner ear. In addition to being the horse's organ of hearing, the ear is also responsible for helping the horse to maintain balance, and the inner ear in particular performs the important basic function of letting the brain know the position of the head.

The outer ear is the part we are all familiar with, and even a short time observing horses shows us how extremely mobile the outer ear is. This easily visible part of the ear, an erect cartilaginous portion, is the *pinna*. This can be moved in all directions to enable the horse to hear all around, and each ear moves independently so the horse can listen in two different directions at once. Attached to the head, the pinna becomes a funnel shape at its base, then travels down into the skull where it makes a 90-degree turn forward to meet the *eardrum*. Made of a thin membrane, the eardrum separates the outer and middle parts of the ear and is connected to three small bones. These bones are named for their shapes, being the hammer, anvil, and stirrup (or malleus, incus, and stapes), and they are the method by which sound is conveyed to the inner ear.

The middle ear is lined with a mucus membrane and connected to the throat (pharynx) by the Eustachian tube which enables the middle ear pressure to be regulated to match the external atmosphere. The opening to the throat is protected by a flap of cartilage which only opens when swallowing (think of how swallowing can help your own ears "pop"). Horses and donkeys (and, strangely, also a species of tree shrew) possess a large pouch-like structure on each Eustachian tube. This is known as the *guttural pouch* and is comprised of paired air sacs located between the pharynx and floor of the skull. These air sacs are closely related to a great many cranial nerves and blood vessels, and these may be impacted by diseases or infections of the guttural pouch.

Two "windows" of membrane separate the middle and inner ear, and the stirrup bone is attached to the upper of these two membranous windows. This is the mechanism by which soundwaves reaching the eardrum are transmitted through to the inner ear. The inner ear is known as the labyrinth due to its complicated shape. This shape is necessary as the labyrinth fits in among the bones of the skull. The inner ear is made up of a series of membranous tubes with many nerve endings within their linings. The entirety of the inner ear is filled with a fluid called endolymph. The main cavity of the labyrinth is the vestibule. For simplicity, the anatomy of the inner ear may be considered two groups of tubular compartments. The lower of these curls around almost like the shell of a snail and is called the *cochlea*. Hearing occurs when the soundwaves being transmitted through the bones of the middle ear create a resonance which moves the endolymph within the cochlea. The second set of compartments is comprised of three semicircular channels, each of which are arranged at 90 degrees to one another. These compartments share endolymph circulation with the vestibule. The movement of the endolymph within these channels serves to relay positional changes of the head through to the brain, assisting in balance and spatial awareness.

Chapter 6

Health Care and Monitoring

THIS is another subject where many, *many* detailed books are available. My personal favorite is *Veterinary Notes for Horse Owners* by M. Horace Hayes (originally published some 140 years ago, 1877 to be exact, but updated and revised many times over the years) and Lt. Col. W. S. Codrington's *Know Your Horse in Health and Disease*, first published in 1955, and also updated on a number of occasions. Hayes's book is incredibly detailed, but there are some pretty basic, important things to know as a novice horse owner, so I'll cover them for you here. First, let's discuss the all-important first aid kit.

First Aid Kit

I recommend keeping a few basic tools and supplies in your first aid kit, and keeping them all neatly together. A plastic storage box with a lid is ideal as it keeps everything together and is easily accessible. So, what goes into that plastic box?

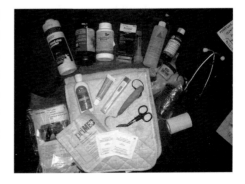

- **Thermometer:** The digital kind make life easier, but just make sure to check/replace the battery regularly.
- **Stethoscope:** Maybe not *vital* but they are very useful and not expensive, so worth having.
- **Hoof pick:** Yes, I know we all have plenty of those, but it's useful to keep one on hand in your first aid kit when dealing with a problem instead of having to go get one from your grooming kit.
- **Blood stop powder:** Just like it sounds, a fine powder that helps stop bleeding. I like it for scrapes which aren't really *bleeding* but just seeping blood. (Plus, adhesive bandages really don't stick on hairy animals!)
- **Antiseptic cream:** There are a lot of these available, some with added fly repellent. I personally like Corona as it's not terribly expensive and does the job.
- **Liniment:** I usually go for the kind that goes on cool then heats to soothe, but it's all personal preference.
- **Cotton balls or cotton pads:** I buy the ones meant for removing makeup.
- **Cohesive ("Vetrap") bandage**
- **Scissors:** The type without points are usually safest for use with horses as they have a habit of moving at the most inopportune moments, and the last thing you want to do is make a minor problem worse by stabbing your horse! Alternatively, you can buy scissors which have bent blades, specifically for cutting through bandages without cutting through skin at the same time.
- **Epsom salts:** Good for soaking hoof abscesses and can also be added to bran mash.
- **Saline solution:** I like to keep a bottle of this on hand because it's useful for cleaning wounds, either by squirting directly onto the wound or using with cotton pads. I just buy a bottle of cheap contact lens saline and use that.
- **Stable bandages and pads**
- **Gauze dressing pads**

- **Corner piece of a plastic feed bag:** This can be used to hold on a foot poultice if you don't have a poultice boot.
- **Tweezers:** These are vital for easy removal of ticks. Just get the tips of the tweezers down as far as you possibly can around the tick's head and give a good, hard yank! Always remember to check the tick to make sure you got it all, as leaving the head or mouth in the skin can lead to infection.

You may have noticed that I didn't mention medication or painkillers. I don't believe that medication should be given without veterinary advice first being sought, and if you are a novice horse owner, you should contact your vet if your horse is exhibiting pain to a degree where you think painkilling drugs are required before giving your horse even a mild painkiller such as bute (phenylbutazone) or banamine.

There are a lot of other things you *could* keep in your first aid kit, but these are the most-used items. As a matter of good practice, you should check over your kit every month or two, just to make sure nothing is missing. Sometimes even when you don't recall using it, you may have grabbed something from there intending to return it but never did. Better to notice the missing item when it's convenient to replace it and *not* when dealing with a problem.

A final thought on the supplies for your first aid kit. As I previously mentioned, whenever you add the word "horse" or "equine" to an item, the price goes up, and a lot of items are easily found elsewhere. Check out your local dollar store or supermarket for things like gauze, cotton pads, and even antiseptic cream. A couple of vets have recommended using a human triple antibiotic cream like Neosporin for small wounds (it does a good job and, unlike my favorite Corona, it doesn't keep wounds open), and you can pick up a tube of the generic version with the same ingredients for a dollar or less!

Temperature, Pulse, and Respiration

First thing to know is "TPR," or temperature, pulse, and respiration. You need to know how to check each of these, and you also need to know what is normal for *your* horse. As a quick example, the first time I checked the temperature on a poorly horse after moving to Florida, I panicked just a little for a moment because his temperature seemed quite high. Then, I considered the fact of the Florida climate and decided to compare his temperature to some other horses to give me a baseline to compare. I could then see that, yes this horse's temperature was elevated, but only a degree or so over the others (which was certainly more reassuring than when I *thought* he had a fever of five or six degrees above "normal"). So, like I said, know *your* horse's normal ranges.

Temperature

The textbook normal temperature is 99–101.5ºF (37.2–38.6ºC). The horse's temperature is normally taken rectally. Digital thermometers make life much easier for the person involved. Make sure that the thermometer is switched on, and it helps if you coat the tip with petroleum jelly. Standing to the side of the horse in case of kicking (how would you like someone sticking a thermometer there?), grasp the tail at the dock, and pull it toward you. Many horses will resist this, and you'll find that their dock muscles are pretty strong, but just be gentle and persistent until you can see the horse's anus. Slide the thermometer gently into the horse's anus (I usually find that rotating the thermometer tip back and forth makes this easier), then press it to one side so the metal bulb on the tip is against the rectal wall. Hold it there until the thermometer beeps to signal the reading is complete, then withdraw the thermometer and read the displayed temperature. If you are using an old-fashioned mercury thermometer, you should shake it two or three times before use, then proceed in the same way with lubrication and insertion. The usual practice with these is to hold it in place for sixty seconds or until you can see that the mercury line has stopped moving before withdrawing and checking the temperature. Not only are digital thermometers more accurate, but they will generally give a quicker result. Regardless of which kind you use, make sure to only insert the thermometer about half of its length and keep a good grip on it! If you've ever wondered why horse people often have a piece of string through the little hole on the end of a mercury thermometer . . . it's there so you don't lose your grasp on it and have the thermometer disappear into the horse (it has been known to happen)!

Pulse

Normal resting pulse is between twenty-eight to forty-four beats per minute. The usual way of taking the pulse is using your fingertips on the inside of the jaw (on either side). The alternative method is to use a stethoscope just behind the elbow. Once you locate the pulse point, count the beats while using a stopwatch, even on your phone, with a second hand to time for fifteen seconds. Multiply the pulse beats by four to get the beats per minute (or count beats for thirty seconds and just double the result). The pulse should feel strong and even. *Never* use your thumb to check a pulse, as your own thumb has a fairly strong pulse beat of its own and you may easily mistake that for the horse's pulse.

Respiration

Normal resting respiration is ten to twenty-four breaths per minute. This is the easiest vital sign to check. Just watch the horse's side and count each breath as the sides swell. Again, use a stopwatch to count for one minute.

Signs of Good/Poor Health

So, why is it important to know how to check these vital signs, and also to know what they *should* be? Well, a sick horse may have a fever, rapid pulse, or rapid breathing. A weak, thready pulse, even if the beats per minute are within the normal range, could also indicate illness. A lower than normal temperature could be an indicator of shock. Always remember that these signs should be taken alongside other more general signs of good and poor health. In this regard, keeping your horse at home allows you to really know what is normal behavior for your horse, so an alert horse owner will pick up on changes which they may have missed if their horse was stabled elsewhere with someone else dealing with daily care.

While the following list of signs of good/poor health may seem dauntingly long, remember that the majority of these signs are things which most horse owners, no matter how inexperienced, will notice automatically. If you can't recall noticing any of them, you may have automatically noted them as normal, and so disregarded. A little like when you travel a very familiar route, you may reach your destination without any recollection of a section of road you traveled, because nothing out of the ordinary occurred.

So, what signs should we be looking for?

- **Attitude:** The first thing you will notice. In general, horses will have an alert and interested demeanor. If your horse usually greets you at the gate with a whinny and happy expression, but today remains where they are and ignores you or is unusually grouchy, that could be an indicator that they aren't feeling 100 percent.

- **Coat:** The coat should be smooth and shiny (even a thick winter coat should look healthy) and not appear dull, dry, or staring (standing on end). Bald patches should be checked carefully as these can be caused by lice or ringworm (which can be transferred to humans), and badly rubbed manes/tails may be caused by "sweet itch" which is an allergic reaction to the saliva of biting flies/midges.

- **Eyes:** A horse's eyes should be bright and clear, with no discharge or excessive tearing. If you pull back the eyelid, the mucus membrane should be moist and salmon-pink in color.

- **Legs:** The horse should appear sound, moving normally and fully weight-bearing on all four legs. Legs should not be swollen or filled and should not have any "hot spots" when touched. Likewise, the hooves should not feel overly warm, though you should bear in mind that a stabled horse's hooves will often be warmer than one who is out at pasture. The most important thing is that they should all feel the same. If one foot is much hotter than the others, that usually indicates a problem.

- **Nose:** There should be no discharge from the nose. A little wetness may be normal, but a very snotty nose or dirty/foul smelling discharge should be cause for concern.

- **Breathing:** A horse's breathing should be deep and even and should not have excessive noise (of course, if your horse is already known to have noisy breathing, often called roaring or whistling, then this would be "normal" for your horse). No excessive coughing. Like humans, the occasional cough due to dust or dryness is normal, but persistent coughing should be investigated.

- **Droppings:** If you're new to horse ownership, you will soon find that you seem to take an inordinate interest in what your horse leaves behind. As horse people, we tend to have a great fascination with our horses' toilet habits, and this can seem weird at first. Don't worry, we all do it (though you will find that non-horse people look at you strangely if they overhear a conversation about the texture/feel of a horse's droppings)! Generally, each ball of dung should be well-formed and should break on hitting the ground. Very dry droppings could mean the horse has been constipated. Very loose droppings could be a concern, however it is also fairly common for this to happen if the horse is grazing a lot of new, young grass, so consider any potential dietary causes before getting too worried. Some mares will have quite wet droppings when they come into heat, but again, this would be something you will come to know as "normal" for a particular horse. The horse should not appear to strain excessively to pass droppings.

- **Urine:** This can be more difficult to monitor, but if you see your horse urinating, the urine should be pale/clear in color and not very smelly. Some horses are quite particular about where they will urinate (I knew a pony who *hated* to urinate outside and would try to hold it until he was put into his stall if at all possible), so if they hold back then the urine will likely be very yellow or dark in color and possibly quite pungent. Again, "normal" is relative to your horse. As with droppings, the horse should not appear to be experiencing difficulty in passing urine.

- **Appetite:** A healthy horse will tend to eat all of their feed, though if you are overfeeding them, this can cause a loss of appetite (imagine going to an all-you-can-eat buffet for every single meal; you would soon lose the enjoyment of eating). If your horse is "quidding" or dropping partially chewed food, there may be a problem with their teeth and this should be checked out.

Broadly speaking, those are the signs of good health. Pretty obviously, the signs of ill health are basically the opposites. A listless horse, or one who is lame. A coughing horse or one with a snotty, runny nose. If you suspect that your horse is off-color, this would be a reason to do some further examination. Check those vital signs, TPR. Fortunately, most horses are, generally speaking, as healthy as . . . well, the phrase "healthy as a horse" had to come from somewhere! Most horses can sustain various injuries (and some of them seem to take delight in finding novel and mysterious ways of hurting themselves), but other than that, the thing most commonly getting owners to grab a phone to call the vet is colic.

Colic

Colic is a word that strikes fear into the heart of most horse owners, and I think that is partly due to the knowledge that it can be serious, but also due to the fact that there's so little we can actually *do* about it. We feel comforted when we are able to do something. We can wash and medicate cuts, we can cold-hose bruises or swellings, but colic isn't something we can *do* much about by ourselves. Colic can be very serious, and can necessitate surgery or even cause death. Having said that (and after probably scaring you half to death), I'll give you an even scarier number. It's estimated that 64,000 horses worldwide die from colic (or are euthanized as a result) per year. Now, that is a horribly high number, but when you consider there are an estimated 58,372,100 domestic horses in the world, that works out to be about 0.1 percent or one in a thousand. Bear in mind that often the decision to euthanize or operate comes down to financial considerations since a *routine* colic surgery will probably set you back anywhere from $2,000 to $5,000. More complicated procedures will obviously be more costly. If the surgeon opens up your horse, they may still not be able to save them, which leaves you with a vet bill of several thousand dollars which needs to be paid. This is one of the major reasons to try to insure your horse so that hopefully you can make the decision rationally. Are you willing/able to spend that kind of money when there is absolutely no guarantee of success? With that said, the vast majority of horses who colic will not need surgery. In fact, many of them will get through it just fine without any human intervention, they get colicky in the night, they roll a bit, it gets better, they're up and waiting for breakfast without any evidence of a problem (except maybe they're a bit dirtier than usual).

So, what symptoms would make you think your horse has colic? The first thing you may notice is that your horse appears generally uneasy, perhaps continually looking around at their flanks and/or kicking up at their belly. The horse may paw the ground, often quite violently, and may lie down. Once down, they may roll/thrash around. There may also be patchy sweating.

Another thing to be aware of is whether your horse is eating and if they seem to be passing droppings normally. If the colic involves a blockage somewhere in the gut, then peristalsis, the constant movement of the digestive tract which moves food all the way from mouth to rectum, will continue to work, meaning that the gut *after* the blockage will continue to work until the horse has pooped out all that is in there. This then leaves the gut empty, and as it is held in its rather complicated position just by being full, you are now left with a substantial amount of empty gut sort of flopping around like an empty sausage skin. It used to be thought that a horse rolling violently when this happened was the cause of "twisted gut," when the empty gut flips around and tangles, but modern veterinary science has shown that this is not the case. A torsion (twisted gut) will *cause* the severe pain that the horse tries to relieve by rolling, but rolling doesn't cause the torsion. (Regardless of the actual cause, a twisted gut is *not* a good thing.) If possible, and if you can do it without getting hurt by an agitated horse, you could check the capillary refill and check for gut sounds. (If your horse is so agitated that you cannot safely do this, I recommend calling your vet right away.) The capillary refill is easy to check. Simply lift your horse's lip and press a finger briefly against their gums (which should be a pink color in a healthy horse). The pink color should return almost immediately when you remove your finger. A "cap" refill of over two seconds is a definite cause for concern.

Checking gut sounds is also quite straightforward. You can use a stethoscope if you have one, but usually I just press my ear to the horse. I tend to listen just in front of the hip bone on each side and also just in front of the stifle on each side. With horse gut sounds, gurgles are good and silence is bad! Again, please be careful doing this, because if the horse already has pain there and you are pressing on the painful area, they may kick.

When it comes to colic, I advise that you err on the side of caution. If the colic/pain seems mild, then monitor closely, but if in *any* doubt, *call the vet!* Yes, you may end up with a bill for a call-out which wasn't really necessary, but that's still far better than waiting too long and either facing surgery or, even worse, losing your horse. When you speak to the vet, try to be calm and practical. Tell them the symptoms, how long it has been going on, and your observations. If you were able to check cap refill, gut sounds, temperature, etc., tell them those, too. Accurate information will help your vet decide whether to get to you ASAP or to advise that you monitor and call back if things get worse. Remember, you are not the vet's only client, and they have to prioritize even emergency calls; a horse with a bleeding artery, for example, will need to be attended to more quickly than one with mild colic. Unless instructed to do so by the vet, do *not* give your horse any medication (not even if Facebook tells you to)! You may just make the vet's job more difficult, leading us neatly on to our next section: when to call the vet.

When to Call the Vet

When *should* you call the vet out? This is both really easy and really difficult to answer. The obvious answer is that you should call the vet when they are needed, but the level of problem that necessitates the vet will depend somewhat upon your own experience and knowledge. I'll say it again: if in doubt, *call*. Hopefully your vet will, as mine does, be willing to give advice over the phone. This is one of the definite downsides to keeping your horse at home, since at a boarding stable you will generally be able to ask someone with more experience for their thoughts. Again, Facebook is *not* a substitute for professional advice or at least a real, live person who can actually physically *see* your horse. I've been stunned by some of the symptoms described in online posts seeking advice (I remember one which said "my horse has had liquid diarrhea for two days, what can I give him to help?" Uh . . . *what*?!). Usually the unanimous response has been "get off Facebook and *call the vet!*"

Some of the more common problems that would necessitate a call to the vet are:

- **Major wounds/bleeding:** If bleeding is profuse or the area injured is extensive and likely to require stitches, or if the horse is bleeding heavily, try to stem the flow by applying pressure to the wound while you wait for the vet to arrive. Also, any wounds which are affecting a joint are in danger of damaging the joint capsule, a sort of protective bubble filled with synovial fluid which lubricates the joint. If the joint capsule is damaged, this important fluid may be lost, creating more serious problems.
- **Colic**

- **Sudden/severe lameness:** I have usually found with my own horses that a sudden and severe lameness has been due to a hoof abscess (and if you find the lame foot to be very warm in a spot, that is another indicator of an abscess). A frequent cause of hoof abscesses is a puncture wound to the sole of the foot, often by a horse treading on a nail or similar sharp object. Unfortunately, unless you actually find the offending object still in the foot, these wounds are very small and will very often heal over before you even see them, and this is where problems can arise. The surface wound may heal, but the penetrating injury has forced dirt and bacteria into the hoof capsule where it forms an infection and abscess. As the hoof capsule is a rather confined and hard-edged area, the swelling of the abscess can cause extreme pain. If you *do* find your horse with a nail or similar object still embedded in their foot, you at least have the chance to get ahead of the problem and may want to contact your vet even before removing the object.

- **Sudden/severe swelling, particularly of limbs:** Even a very minor wound may become infected, and sometimes this can lead to cellulitis, a bacterial infection that causes major swelling to the affected limb. (I have just dealt with a serious case of this, which is why it has made it onto this list. A very minor injury, tiny enough that it had escaped notice, caused my thoroughbred's foreleg swell to almost twice its normal girth from elbow to fetlock.) Treatment of cellulitis will generally require antibiotics along with anti-inflammatory drugs, so veterinary attention will definitely be required.

- **Eye injuries:** These can cause major swelling, so even if the actual eye isn't affected, veterinary treatment/medication may be needed.

- **Mouth injuries:** As with humans, horse mouths can bleed heavily if injured, and obviously an injury can affect the horse's ability to eat, so if you think they have injured their mouth you should probably contact the vet.

- **Disorientation:** While it seems really, *really* obvious, if your horse cannot stand/falls over/is walking into things/has an apparent broken bone, *call the vet!*

- **Choke:** This is when the horse has something blocking their throat and cannot swallow, evidenced by drooling, distress, and perhaps even a visible lump in their esophagus.

Treatment of Minor Injuries

Horses seem to find an inexhaustible supply of things to injure themselves with, so after the initial panicking and treatment of the resultant wounds, we get to spend hours wondering *how on earth did they do that?* In addition to the first aid kit already covered, the single most useful thing for treating most minor problems is a garden hose supplying lots of clean, cold water. Horse has a cut? Hose it clean first. Swollen leg? Hose it. Bruise? Hose it. A little bit like the joke that a tool kit needs only duct tape and WD-40. (If it moves but it shouldn't, use duct tape. If it doesn't move but it should, use WD-40.) The benefits of plain running water are often underestimated. A conscientious horse owner should, as already stated, know what is normal for *their* horse, and that includes knowing if they usually have any lumps, bumps, or filled (swollen) legs. You should get in the habit, at least once a day, of giving your horse a quick once-over to check for anything untoward: lumps, bumps, and general boo-boos. You should obviously be picking their feet at least once per day, so this is the ideal time to check for heat or anything else abnormal since you're already running your hands down their legs.

Along with the cold running water, the other most important thing you can use when faced with an equine emergency is your common sense. Ever read the book *The Hitchhiker's Guide to the Galaxy* (or seen the movie, but the book is so much better!)? Well, remember what it says right on the front of the guide. *Don't panic!* Yes, it's frightening to see your "baby" bleeding or in pain, and horses can bleed a *lot*. Yes, I freely admit to panicking just a little when my foal yanked a tooth loose playing with the fencing and stood with a tooth hanging out and blood pouring from his mouth. When I called my vet, his wonderfully common-sense, calm response was "It happens. Should fall out on its own, or if you can get a grip on it, twist and yank it out. Give me a call if it's still hanging in there tomorrow." To finish the story, I calmed down, mostly due to my vet's reaction, and after a little while when it was apparent that the flappy tooth was making it hard for the foal to suckle, I did as I was instructed. Now, at not quite one year old, my colt's big boy tooth is already through in that spot. But my point is, no matter how experienced you are, sometimes things still make you panic a little bit, and that's fine. It's how you *deal* with them that matters, so go ahead and panic a bit, freak out a little for a

minute, then get on with dealing with the problem. Most times, you'll wash away that river of blood to find a tiny cut (and if you have a pale-colored horse, a grey, or palomino, blood looks *way* worse than on a darker coat!). Small cuts/scrapes should be cleaned carefully, using that oh-so-important water, and if necessary, treated with blood stop or antiseptic. In all honesty, small cuts/scrapes would most likely heal up just fine by themselves, but it's human nature to feel like we should do *something*, and smearing on a blob of antiseptic won't hurt. (And if it's not a *small* cut, see the previous chapter!) In summer especially I will usually spray fly repellent around a wound after cleaning, just as an added precaution.

If you keep more than one horse, chances are that at some point they'll get into a fight. Usually the fight won't do a whole lot of damage (unless stallions are involved, but I do *not* recommend *any* novice owner having a stallion!). Most of the time one or both horses will end up with some nice bruises from kicks etc., and a little treatment can ease these. Guess what treatment? Yep, you guessed it, cold water. In the old days we would talk of cold-hosing a bruise or swelling. These days people talk about hydrotherapy. I guess it sounds better/more technical, but it's the same thing. Cold water hosed over the bruise should help minimize swelling, but really nature just needs to take its course. If the swelling is very large or hard, or persists for days, or concerns you in some way, give the vet a call. It may be that some other treatment is needed which the vet can advise you on even though their actual attendance may not be needed. When you are cold-hosing a bruise/swelling, use the water on as firm a jet as your horse will tolerate and keep the water moving around the affected area. This tends to be more effective than a gentle trickle, but obviously increase the pressure slowly. (That cellulitis I mentioned above? Take a wild guess how I'm treating it while waiting for the vet . . . Yep. Cold-hosing!)

Though it's not exactly an injury, you should be prepared to deal with a twisted shoe, if your horse wears shoes, as your farrier isn't on call in the same way as a vet. In many ways, while it is more expensive to replace a lost shoe, if the shoe comes all the way off it usually creates fewer problems than when they twist. When a shoe becomes loose and gets twisted off one side of the hoof, there is always a great danger that the protruding nails will hurt the horse, either by being stepped on and puncturing the sole or by hurting the adjacent leg. I have heard a lot of people in Florida complain about muddy turnouts "sucking" the shoes off a horse's feet, and I truly don't believe that happens. A horseshoe is attached to the foot by seven or eight nails with the ends neatly hooked down. I cannot imagine mud strong enough to pull those loose. What I *can* imagine quite easily is a horse's foot slipping in that mud so that their own hind toe levers the shoe from the front foot! Either way, if your horse is shod even just on the front feet, it would be a good idea to invest in a shoe puller, basically a very heavy duty set of pincers which are designed to make shoe removal easier. Having tried over the years with regular pliers etc., it *is* possible to get a shoe off without the proper tools, but they can be pretty inexpensive and well worth adding to your horse-related tool kit. The correct way to remove a shoe is to work from the heel end but I strongly recommend that you have your farrier show you how to perform this task correctly rather than trying to learn from reading about it! I am sure that most if not all farriers would rather spend a few minutes teaching you how to do this than have you calling them in a panic asking them what to do!

Regularly Scheduled "Maintenance"

Of course, here I really mean "maintenance" of your *horse*. Vaccinations, deworming, hoof care, etc. Vaccinations will vary depending on where you are located and also what kind of lifestyle your horse has. A horse who lives at home, without contact with "strange" horses will generally only require vaccinations twice a year, spring and fall. If your horse travels to a lot of competitions or is otherwise in contact with a lot of other horses (even if you trail ride in very popular places), you may need to increase the frequency of vaccinations.

Vaccinations

The vaccinations most commonly given (in the USA) include:

- Tetanus
- Eastern/Western Equine Encephalomyelitis (EEE/WEE)
- Equine Herpesvirus (EHV, also known as equine rhinopneumonitis)
- Influenza
- West Nile Virus
- Rabies (unlike in cats and dogs, this vaccination is not a legal requirement but as rabies is a 100 percent fatal disease it makes sense to vaccinate against it)
- Strangles

I know this looks like a scary-long list, but it really isn't as bad as it looks. Most vets will give a single shot which covers the first four on the list, with the West Nile and Rabies shots administered separately (though there are now some combination vaccines which include West Nile with the other diseases). Strangles is given as a sort of nasal spray, but even my own vet says the effectiveness isn't always great (though that could be because neither of us have a death wish to try sticking an eight-inch tube up my mare's nose)! Anyway, your vet is the best person to advise you on the frequency and type of vaccinations most appropriate for your horse, and the website for the American Association of Equine Practitioners (aaep.org) also has many useful links. In many US states it is possible to purchase vaccines and administer them yourself, but this is not something I would recommend for a novice owner. If nothing else, when the vet comes out twice a year or so, they will be able to give you a professional opinion of your horse's condition and answer any minor questions you may have.

Another requirement in the US is that your horse possesses a valid, negative Coggins test. This blood test (named for its developer, Dr. Leroy Coggins) is required for any horse in a boarding facility or any horse being transported. The test checks for the presence of antibodies associated with Equine Infectious Anemia, and any horse which tests positive must be either euthanized or quarantined. If quarantine is chosen, the horse must be branded to identify its infected status and must then be kept a *minimum* of

880 yards (a half mile) from any other horse for the rest of its life. A positive test is quite rare and most owners choose to have an infected horse euthanized rather than condemn them to a solitary existence. You should *never* purchase a horse which does not have a current valid Coggins certificate.

Deworming

Why do we need to deworm our horses? Well, a horse with a worm burden may tend to have trouble maintaining good condition, or may be more susceptible to colic and other health issues. The parasite life cycle, in very simple terms, starts with the horse eating parasite larvae while grazing. The parasites grow to maturity inside the horse and lay their eggs. The horse poops out the eggs onto the pasture where they develop and hatch into larvae which the horse then eats while grazing, and on and on and on.

While we know that parasite control is important for horse health, deworming has become something of a contentious topic these days. In the old days, we would deworm our horses every six to eight weeks, rotating the type of dewormer to maximize effectiveness (as different chemicals kill different parasites) and minimize the chances of parasites becoming resistant to the chemicals. Many people nowadays prefer to carry out Fecal Egg Counts, which are about as simple as they sound. You take a sample of poop and send it off to a lab to have the number of parasite eggs counted. Now, no eggs doesn't necessarily equal no parasites, so these counts may be of limited value. Veterinary opinions I have read seem to say that Fecal Egg Reduction Counts are more useful, i.e. do a count before deworming, then again ten to fourteen days after deworming, and compare the results. If egg count has decreased, the deworming helped. If egg count has not decreased, then the dewormer used was ineffective (due to resistance to the chemical) and that dewormer should not be used again on that horse. To be honest, I still prefer the old route, though I don't deworm quite so frequently, perhaps four times per year, using different chemicals each time. The best method of parasite reduction (I'm quite sure that every horse, no matter how frequently treated, carries some parasite burden) is prevention, so get out there and pick up as much poop from the field as you can! If you bring a new horse to your property, deworm them and keep them in a stall/confined area for a couple of days so that if they pass parasites, they aren't spreading them around the field.

As with vaccinations, I recommend discussing deworming practices with your vet, as needs vary depending on where in the country you live. Places like southern California or desert-type environments are not welcoming for parasites, so the need for deworming is lower. Your local equine vet will be most familiar with the situation in your area. (Yes, you could also ask at the local feed store, but bear in mind that they sell dewormers and so have an interest in you using them!)

As a basic guide, below is a list of the main dewormer chemicals (which are obviously all sold under a variety of brand names) and the parasites they are intended to control.

Dewormer	Parasites
Pyrantel Pamoate	Large and small strongyles, pinworms, roundworms
Fenbendazole/oxibendazole	Large and small strongyles, pinworms, roundworms
Ivermectin	Large and small strongyles, pinworms, ascarids, hairworms, large-mouth stomach worms, bots, lungworms, intestinal threadworms (Ivermectin also controls summer sores caused by bots and dermatitis from neck threadworms)
Praziquantel	Tapeworms (Praziquantel is generally found in combination with Ivermectin)

Hoof Care

Hoof care varies somewhat from horse to horse, but the basic rule has always been that horses should receive a farrier visit every six weeks. This assumes that there are no problems which make it necessary for the hooves to be attended to more frequently. Whether barefoot or shod, the hooves need to be trimmed and shaped to minimize cracking. Your job as horse owner is obviously to keep the feet clean, by picking them out at least once per day. This will minimize problems like thrush, which thrives in warm, damp environments like unpicked feet, especially along the deep clefts at the sides of the frog. Your farrier is the best person to advise on whether barefoot or shod is best for your horse. Even if you prefer a horse to have natural, bare feet, it isn't always the best thing for them, and your preferences are less important than the welfare of the animal. Yes, shoeing is more expensive than barefoot, but it's cheaper than constant vet attention due to lameness, or having a horse who is no more than a lawn ornament due to foot pain making them unrideable.

Grooming

Regular grooming is good for removal of dead hair, keeping your horse looking good, and stimulating their circulation as well as being a nice bonding time for you both. Another benefit of grooming is that you will be touching all over your horse and will get to know their lumps and bumps, and will quickly notice anything out of the ordinary. In an ideal world we would do this every day, but I know that daily life gets in the way. At the very least, pick their feet every day and try to give a quick groom, but if weekends are the only time you can give a thorough grooming, so be it. Baths can be given when the weather permits (would *you* like to be given an outdoor bath on a cold, breezy day?), and I've found over the years that there is no need to pay what can be quite high prices for special equine shampoos and conditioners. I tend to use whatever I can get in the biggest bottle at the dollar store and have never had any problems. As an aside, if like me you have a pale colored horse (my QH is palomino) then you will find that regular baths or at the very least tail washings are a must. If (like my horse!) you find that the bottom of the tail has become very stained (we have a pond that she likes to play in), before you spend a lot on special whitening shampoos, try this destaining method I have had great success with: Wet down the tail, then make a paste out of blue/original Dawn dish soap and baking soda. Rub that liberally into the length of the tail where it is stained and let it sit while you wet/shampoo/rinse the rest of the horse. Rinse the tail out, then use a whitening shampoo if you like, or just condition the tail well and rinse.

Things like mane pulling, tail trimming, face/bridle path/leg trimming are all entirely optional and to an extent will depend upon what you do with your horse. If possible, I like to leave their legs untrimmed, as that little tuft of hair that grows on the back of the fetlock seems to encourage water to drip *behind* the horse's heels rather than onto the heel area, and it is my personal opinion that this is why none of my horses suffer from cracked heels. I also tend to take part in shows where my horses are not judged solely on how they look (i.e. dressage, etc.) so I choose not to trim off their whiskers. In

Germany it is actually illegal under Animal Welfare Law to remove a horse's whiskers (or to clip the hair from the inside of their ears). Another aside, the horse's whiskers serve the same purpose as a cat's: they tell the horse where their head will fit! I know an owner who would trim away their horse's whiskers *and* the long "feeler" hairs around the eyes before shows, and those horses invariably came home with cuts/scrapes on their faces because they would stick their heads in places they shouldn't! There is also research stating that horse whiskers are an essential part of their system. After all, when you consider that a horse cannot see directly in front of themselves, it makes sense that the whiskers form an integral part of their sensory apparatus.

Chapter 7

Maintenance of Property and Pastures

NOW that you have the perfect home for your horse, what do you need to keep it perfect? This should be a fairly short chapter, but I'm sure you've already noticed that I'm not good at "short" answers to anything, so here goes. Maintenance of your property/pastures really has two main purposes: to keep things clean and to keep things safe. Now, by clean I don't mean you need to be pressure washing fences every week. I mean clean from your horse's viewpoint. You guessed it, pick up that poop! If at all possible, at least once per week go out and pick up as much poop from the field as you can. Think of it as a weekly workout (or if you have kids, send them out to do it)! If you work five days a week, this will most likely be a weekend chore for you. Take it from me, it really is worth sacrificing maybe a half day to do all of your barn maintenance chores. Pick up the poop and dispose of it wherever you dispose of your stall cleaning muck. Empty out water buckets and scrub them thoroughly. Scrub out feed buckets.

Something else to consider is mowing your pastures. Yes, your horse will do their best to graze down the grass, but they are very picky about what they eat, which means that weeds will be left untouched and allowed to flower/seed/grow more weeds. It may be necessary to run over the field periodically with a riding mower or similar (trust me, you do *not* want to be mowing a field using a push mower!). Even a field specifically seeded for grazing will develop weeds over time as birds and animals drop seeds on their travels. Weeds seem to have a much greater will to live than grass, so if you give them half a chance they will take over and monopolize the water and nutrients from the soil, leaving your grass to struggle. Driving on the grass a little can also help it to grow as it crushes the growing tips of the leaves which encourages them to "tiller," or split and form extra leaves.

To keep your property safe, check your fences (which can be done from horseback if you like) for damaged/broken boards/loose wire. Check your stables/shelters for any damaged boards or doors. Make sure that gates are secure. If you find something that needs to be fixed, *do it*. Don't just make a mental note to do it "when you have time." Unless it's something that you can't fix right away (i.e. a broken board when you have no spares and will have to buy some), just do it now. When horses are involved, things have a way of escalating. That board your horse kicked and broke in the stall could very easily become that board your horse kicks again, getting their leg stuck and leading to injuries and vet bills! An ounce of prevention is worth a pound of cure!

Trailer Care

A few notes on this important piece of equipment:

- Keep the tires covered while stored. Sunlight is not kind to tires, so keeping them covered with even a couple of pieces of tarp will minimize dry rot.
- Regularly check the floor for integrity and strength. It should go without saying that you must clean out the trailer after every use. Piles of rotting poop are *not* good for trailer floors!
- Check wiring and lights before every use.
- Check brakes before every use.
- Have the wheel hubs/axles checked and lubricated per manu-facturer's instructions.
- If the trailer is stored for an extended period of time, try to at least move it around on your property occasionally to keep things from seizing up.

- Check/lubricate hinges and catches on doors and partitions.
- Make sure you have a spare wheel and appropriate method of raising the trailer. Make sure the spare is good!

Safety Precautions

Security

If you are going to be home most of the time, you will of course be able to keep an eye on things yourself. But, let's face it, nobody is *always* home. If at

all possible, I recommend installing security cameras to cover property access points/field gates and barn access if applicable. Not only does this let you keep a better watch over your property and horses, but you will have a recording if anything *does* happen. These days, security camera systems are fairly inexpensive, and most can be connected to an app for remote viewing on your cell phone or computer. The photograph above is of an older system, and current ones are of an even higher resolution. One thing you must bear in mind though, especially if you intend to install these yourself, is that "wireless" cameras *do* still require power cables! Also, wireless systems work best with direct line of sight from cameras to DVR.

Fire Safety

As for fire safety, this is basic common sense. Keep things clean and tidy. Try to keep on top of spider webs and the like. Make sure rodents aren't chewing on any electric cables. Keep a couple of fire extinguishers in the barn/hay area, and this shouldn't need to be said, but *no smoking around the barn!*

Protection of Yourself and Others

If you are going to be handling your horse, please make sure to wear proper footwear. Flip-flops and horse feet don't mix well (google some images if you don't believe me!). I will admit to being guilty of wearing sandals or flip-flops when I go out to feed, but if I'm going to be handling a horse I will always have on closed footwear of some sort: sneakers/paddock boots/ rain boots (which look wonderful with a bathrobe!).

If anyone is going to ride or handle your horses (and I mean *anyone*, including family or friends), I strongly recommend having them sign a safety waiver. There are many of these freely available online, and they simply make it clear that the person riding is aware of the dangers inherent in being around horses and is absolving you of any liability. I also would not allow anyone, regardless of how experienced they
are or say they are, to ride without wearing a helmet (this is actually a legal requirement for anyone under sixteen anyway)!

My final thought is on the subject of other people's horses. I'm sure that many people keeping their horses at home have at least considered offering to board horses for others, whether friends or strangers. I strongly suggest that if you *do* decide to take care of someone else's horse, even a friend's or family member's, that you draw up a contract for provision of boarding. This can lay out what they expect of you and what you expect of them, i.e. are they going to buy their own hay and grain? Are they responsible for cleaning their own stall/assisting with paddock-poop-picking? What about if there is an emergency? There is a big difference between caring for your own horse and someone else's.

Routines

If, like me, you have a tendency to be easily sidetracked into dealing with other things, it never hurts to have a routine checklist. Pick up a cheap notice board, or write/print up a checklist and keep it somewhere you'll see every day. You don't need to go to the extent of checking things off (unless you plan on giving yourself gold stars for effort) but it will help you remember the minutiae of things you have to do. Here's what mine typically looks like:

Daily
Feed horses
Clean stalls

Check/fill waters
Pick feet
Groom

Weekly
Pick poop from field
Clean feed/water buckets
Check fences, etc.
Buy feed/hay (depending on your storage situation, you may be able to do this monthly instead)

Monthly
Empty, scrub, and refill field troughs

Chapter 8

Potential Problems
(What Could Go Wrong?)

Behavioral Issues

I think the biggest potential problem when you decide to keep your horse at home is that behavioral issues can develop. Horses are very social creatures, so if you move your horse from an environment where they have a bunch of friends to one where they are living alone (or at least without any four-legged companions), they may become unhappy. If your horse seems particularly upset by having no friends around, but you don't want the additional expense of another horse, some people will bring in a donkey or even a goat/sheep as a companion animal. Just bear in mind that any companion animal will also require proper care from you and whatever veterinary care is required for their species. Donkeys have similar needs to horses, though they are very different animals.

Aggression

Another problem I've encountered is when a previously easygoing horse becomes difficult or even borderline dangerous due to aggression. I've seen this particularly with new horses that have had major changes to their care. For example, a horse which has been used in a riding school or trail riding business, then becomes a one-person horse, may need their feed drastically reduced if their workload shifts from three or four hours per day, six days a week to perhaps one hour, twice a week. Don't be too quick to assume that someone has misrepresented the horse, or, to use the old vernacular, "sold you a pup," until you make sure that you haven't caused the issues yourself. If there *are* inherent dominance or aggression issues, it is quite likely that these stem from the horse being unsure of their position in the "herd" hierarchy. In a one-person, one-horse herd, the alpha, the leader, is *you!* Horses in nature exist in a matriarchal herd structure, and they are truly happiest when someone is in charge of them. When the horse owner/caregiver is nervous and seems submissive to the horse, many horses find this frightening and will react poorly to the situation. Take charge of your horse and you will find that they react positively. It isn't "mean" to have rules for your horse and to enforce those rules firmly. (Firm but fair handling is key.) Over the years I have seen too many horses whose behavior with their owners leaves much to be desired. If you truly feel out of your depth at first, it may be advisable to have a good trainer come out to help you get a grip on the situation before things escalate. In this circumstance, my idea of a "good" trainer is one who works with you and the horse, helping you solve the problems rather than doing it for you. Keep your horse happy and disciplined, and you'll both enjoy the benefits.

Chapter 9

Horse Chart

WHILE it may seem a little overkill to keep a chart if you have only one horse, it is a simple and effective way to keep on top of what your horse's health-care requirements are. Yes, there are apps and online calendars on your phone or computer, but I've always found it just as useful to keep a paper record. Note the date that farrier visits are due and the dates when deworming and vaccinations have been carried out (and what was used). Simple, straightforward, and pretty foolproof. Always try to use your horse's date of birth, or at the very least the year. I have a habit of forgetting an age, so if the horse was twelve when I met them, I then have to remember that I first met them in, say, 2015, so they are now . . . fourteen? More? Put down that they were born in 2003 and it's far easier! The sample chart on the next page will give you a basic idea of what to do. The alternative is to get a planner or calendar and fill it out when things are due. This is fine if you have only one horse or they are all on the same schedule. Just make sure if it's the tear-off type that you don't throw away the old pages!

Sample Chart

	Farrier	Deworming	Vaccinations
Horse Name			
DOB (Year)			
January			
February			
March			
April			
May			
June			
July			
August			
September			
October			
November			
December			

Chapter 10

Other Miscellaneous Thoughts and Suggestions

I needed one more chapter to put the bits and pieces that occurred to me while writing but didn't really merit a whole chapter to themselves (and also didn't really "fit" into any of the other chapters).

Money-Saving Hacks

One thing that seems pretty universal is that keeping horses is *expensive!* It seems like as soon as the word "horse" or "equine" gets attached to something, the price of it goes up (remember what I said about buckets)? Now, obviously there are a lot of things that you really can't get around buying purpose-made, like saddles and bridles and bits etc., but there are also some things you can improvise to save a few bucks here and there. Some of them may take a little ingenuity, or a chunk of time, but they will also save money. A few items you can make for yourself are:

- **Feed scoops:** Old coffee containers, thoroughly washed, make a good option, as do the gallon jugs that you can buy oil in (vegetable oil, not motor oil!). Just make sure the jug is well washed, then cut away the base to make a scoop shape.

- **Jumps:** You can use old tires to make nice little cross-country jumps. Just dig a long narrow trench and sink the tires into it, then pack dirt around. Things like log piles also work well. Always make sure that whatever you use is not going to injure your horse (okay, or you) in the event of a fall. You can also make your own jump standards/uprights fairly easily, then use either round poles or even plastic drainpipes as the poles.

- **Hay nets:** These will take a little bit of time. You need forty old bale strings (I always try to cut my strings by the knot so that they're neater to work with). It's a little complicated to explain, so as a friend of my dad's used to say, "Words fail me. See sketch." Or in this case, photographs. Anyway, in all honesty, hay nets aren't particularly expensive to buy, unless they're the slow feed type, but I do like making my own when I have the

time. Also, what else are you going to do with all those bale strings? Forty strings make up eighteen pairs for the net, three strings to braid for a drawstring, and one to fasten the bottom of the net (and also to hang it from while you work).

The finished article

- **Fly spray:** I like to make my own fly spray because it works out cheaper in the long run. There are lots of recipes online for natural fly sprays etc., but I like using concentrated Permethrin (the fly repellent bit) mixed with Avon Skin So Soft Original and water. The Permethrin, as

I said, repels the flies, and the Skin So Soft smells nice (and doubles as a detangler for manes/tails)! In winter time, when flies aren't so bad, you can mix some Skin So Soft with water and it will do the job all by itself. Just follow the instructions on the Permethrin (usually a half ounce will make a half gallon), then add Skin So Soft (highly precise measure, a good few glugs!) and fill up the spray bottle with water. Just make sure to shake up the bottle before each use.

I'm sure there are lots of other things you could come up with that are fairly easy to do yourself and save a bit of money, so be creative! The biggest thing to remember is that whatever you make is *safe* for you and your horse. Saving a few bucks on making your own "whatever" just to spend much bigger bucks on a vet bill is *not* a saving!

Emergency/Disaster Planning

I've always been a big believer in "plan for the worst, hope for the best," so this section may go on a while! This only came to mind recently, while planning for and recovering from Hurricane Irma. (Fortunately, we had only very minor damage.) First things first. Be prepared. Having stopped at our local Tractor Supply a few days before the storm (for non-storm stuff), I heard from one of their staff that they had just unloaded an entire truckload of generators, almost sixty of them, that sold out *in two hours*. I can't stress enough, the time to make your preparations and plans is *not* in the few days before a storm hits! Make sure that you have plans in your mind and all supplies possible on hand. The one sort of good thing about hurricanes is that there is always warning (unlike tornadoes). The forecast track and intensity may change, but you will usually have at least a few days' warning that one is headed your way.

Should I Stay or Should I Go?

No, it's not a cue for a song (well it is, but that wasn't what I meant). Where you live, as well as the forecasted storm intensity, will direct you to either load up and evacuate or hunker down where you are. Some people will be in a mandatory evacuation zone and will have no choice. If you have to leave, or choose to leave, you will need a trailer to get your horse out with you. Now, bear in mind that in the run-up to a major storm, it isn't going to be easy to find someone willing to haul your horse when they may also need to get their own to safety, so the sooner you make your decision, the better off you'll be. Also, if you are evacuating, remember that many others will have the same idea, so the drive is not going to be fun. Make sure you know *where* you're going (don't just load up and start driving), and make sure you've checked the forecast storm track. No point heading for "Aunt Brenda's place in Georgia" if the storm is going to hit there, too. You would just be exchanging one bad situation for another. Wherever you're going, make sure you are expected and that there is space for you and however many animals you're bringing. Many showgrounds will open their stabling for hurricane evacuees, but you may need to prebook (and it's usually not free!).

If you decide to evacuate, make sure you have enough hay/grain/water for your horse to make the trip, remembering that what is usually a four-or-five-hour drive may take two or three times as long with heavy traffic. While you won't want to give them grain while you're on the road, you will need it when you get to wherever you're going. Remember you could be there for a week or more, depending on when you leave and how badly the storm impacts the roads etc., before getting back home. But all things considered, evacuating might take less planning than staying, so I'm going to cover the hunkering down scenario more thoroughly. Plus, it's what we did, so I have more to say on that subject.

Our reason to stay during Hurricane Irma was that we only had the ability to haul five horses (using both trailers and two trucks), and we have seven horses here. We also have dogs, parakeets, turtles, and chickens (we didn't have the cats at that point), which we would have also needed to transport. Evacuation was never in the cards for us, and we were fortunate that by the time Irma reached us she was "only" a Category 1/2 hurricane.

Preparing Your Property

Safety and security are your two biggest concerns. You should make every effort to have your hurricane supplies ready long before a storm is on the way, but here's a list of preparations, which are basically common sense whether you have livestock or not.

- Make sure anything that could blow around (trash cans, planters, lawn chairs, patio tables) is either physically secured in place or put somewhere secure.

- If your property has trees, make a quick check that no limbs look like they are ready to fall off. Considering Hurricane Irma took down some incredibly old oaks on our neighbor's property, there's not a whole lot you can do to remove tree limbs in those few days before a storm hits, but hopefully you've kept on top of making sure they aren't too close to your house or barn.

- Make a run to the feed store and stock up on hay, bedding, and grain. If the storm is very bad, it's possible that either you won't be able to get to the feed store for a few days *or* that the feed store will not be able to receive any deliveries. No need to go crazy. Maybe just buy next week's supplies early. Bear in mind that if you get a lot of flooding, your horse may have limited grazing available, so extra hay might also be needed.

- If you have a generator, make sure it works! No point finding out it's broken *after* the power goes out. Make sure you have enough fuel for it. Also, if you use well water, make sure the generator has the right outlet to power the pump (some of them have odd-shaped plugs).

- Having a weather radio, or even walkie-talkies with the emergency weather information function, is a great idea.

- Make sure that all water troughs are clean and filled up. It may also be a good idea to clean out a trash can or two and fill those with water. I usually fill them with water with a little bit of disinfectant and let it sit an hour or so, then empty and rinse thoroughly before filling with water. And, of course, make sure that the water-filled trash cans aren't in any danger of blowing over.

- Make sure your first aid kit is filled, and perhaps even bring it into the house if you don't already keep it there. Also, make sure you have your horse's Coggins to hand.

Preparing Your Horse

In case of an emergency or natural disaster, some basic horse supplies to have on hand are:

- Plastic tote to store any ID straps and livestock markers as well as mane tags. That way you know where those essentials are long before they're needed.
- First aid kit
- Flashlights (head lamps are also awesome in this situation)

There is a huge amount of debate over whether horses should be stabled or at pasture during a storm, with competing logics of "If they're in the barn they won't get hit with flying debris and won't escape if the fences are damaged" versus "If they're in the pasture and the barn falls down, they won't be hurt/trapped/killed in there." I truly don't have a "right" answer for this. I really think it is all about personal preference. Our horses stayed in the barn, because our barn roof has hurricane ties and is a well-built, sturdy structure. We also shuttered the windows and closed the doors at one end of the barn. If your barn is already rickety, it may not stand up to the winds, but I'm not going to say which is the correct choice. Assess your own unique situation to make your decision.

Whether your horse stays in or out during a storm, there is still a chance of them escaping, which is why they *must* be identifiable. There are a lot of ways to do this, but the important thing is that you don't use anything that could get your horse tangled up. This means no halters left on unless they're the breakaway type (and if they are the breakaway type, there's no point in putting ID on them in case the halters, you know, *break away*!). I highly recommend mare ID neck straps. They're often sold for mares going to stud, hence the name. If you google "mare ID neck strap" you'll see what I mean. They are made of a heavy plastic, and I used a Dremel tool to engrave our name and telephone numbers into the plastic, then colored in the grooves with permanent marker to make the text more visible. Our horses wore these for three days during Hurricane Irma with no rubbing or problems. I also made small plastic tags (you can use luggage tags or, in a pinch, cut pieces from a PVC binder) which I braided into their manes. My plan was to use livestock marker crayons to write my telephone number on their coats, but I wasn't able to find any, so I took a friend's advice and used nail polish—which worked great. Some people recommend writing on the hooves, but after a storm they could be deep in mud, so the coat worked much better (though it can be pretty difficult to make nail polish visible on dark horses)! Three forms of ID were probably overkill, but better too many than not enough. You can wait until quite soon before a storm hits to get your horse ID marked, but certainly don't wait until the weather is deteriorating. The storm hit us in the night (that was *lots* of fun) and I marked them all up around lunchtime.

The final thing you want to do before the worst of the storm gets to you is make sure all horses have full buckets of water, then *get yourself safe*. I love all of our horses dearly, but when it comes right down to it, your own safety must take precedence. It's not like you can do any more than you have already done, so don't become a casualty yourself (I actually wore my riding helmet when I went to do my final check. The last thing we needed was for a tree branch to come down on my head!). Once the storm has passed, you can go out and check for damage.

Other than that, it's really down to the things you would prepare if you *didn't* have livestock. Water, food, batteries, fuel, flashlights. *Assume* that you'll lose power. Don't have your refrigerator and freezer filled with food that will spoil if you lose power for an extended period of time (ours went out at midnight on Sunday and was restored Friday evening, though we had a generator so we were okay). Make sure you have food for whatever other animals you have, but again, there's no need to go crazy. It's not a zombie apocalypse. It's a storm. Yes, it's scary (especially in the dark when you can't see what's happening), but it passes. The key, as with so many things, is to be prepared.

After the Storm Passes

Once the emergency or disaster is over and it's safe to do so, head outside and check the damage. I was out in the barn with a flashlight around 5:00 a.m. the morning after the storm to make sure everyone was safe and well. Check that all animals are still where they should be and appear uninjured. If your horses are in the barn, make a quick check that the roof appears undamaged.

Storms are strange things. Our rickety little chicken coop which is little more than posts and chicken wire (though we did staple tarps around it to keep out some of the rain) and an aluminum roof was perfectly fine. The tall wood and aluminum car port ten feet from it broke its posts and folded over like paper (it would have been flat on the ground if it hadn't leaned up against a tree). A friend had a large number of trees destroyed, but three cheap beach balls they'd left out by their pool never even moved. Check that structures are safe and that fences are undamaged. If there are overhead power lines in your area/crossing your property, check that those are safe *before* wandering around. If a power line is down, you should *always* assume it is live.

If any animals are injured, give whatever treatment is necessary. If there is anything serious, call your vet, but bear in mind that phone service may be disrupted or that your vet may be getting a lot of calls.

Cleanup

Once you have taken care of any immediate first aid needs (again, we were incredibly lucky and had no injuries at all), your next task is cleanup. If you're cleaning up fallen trees/branches, be sure to keep an eye out for injured wildlife, too. We actually watched a mother squirrel search out and carry away a baby that had obviously been thrown from the nest, but sometimes they will need human help. Be mindful that less-than-friendly wildlife may also take shelter in piles of branches, so wearing heavy work gloves is a smart idea. Even though the storm has passed, branches/structures may be damaged and could still fall, so be aware of your surroundings and keep safe. The other thing that causes many injuries/fatalities is people doing cleanup and using tools they aren't familiar with, like chainsaws, so if you're not familiar with their use I would strongly recommend leaving that stuff to someone who *does* know what they're doing!

This is certainly not an exhaustive summary, but should hopefully give you some useful hints and ideas to appropriately plan for a storm. As I said, plan for the worst and hope for the best. Far better to be overprepared than the alternative.

Chapter 11

Charming Thoughts

THIS section is simply a few posts from my blog Amulet Equine Services (amuletequineservices.weebly.com/blog) which I thought may be a little interesting, a little funny, and hopefully a little informative.

Food for Thought

Sometimes we need to do a complete rethink on what we think we know. For a long time, I've been a huge fan of loose-ring French link snaffles, believing them to be kind and gentle bits. And I'm certainly not saying they aren't—I still think they're great. My QH mare wears an Abracon loose-ring French link when she's ridden English, and she goes wonderfully softly in it, so when I was starting to school our TB mare for dressage, I switched her to this same bit (fortunately they wear the same size). She was okay, but not particularly soft or accepting of the bit. After giving it a couple of sessions and some thought, I tried a different French link bit. Still loose-ring, but with a thicker mouthpiece, as I thought perhaps the mouthpiece of the Abracon was just too slender for her. A little better, but still not the horse I knew she could be.

Even though I knew better, for the final schooling session before our first foray into a dressage show, I switched her bit again, this time to a very thick, heavy, single-jointed snaffle with fulmer cheeks. The difference was almost instant. She was softer and more accepting, and the very annoying habit of suddenly poking her nose/yanking her head forward was almost gone. So, we used the new fulmer snaffle for our dressage outing, and while we didn't do *great*, we did place in both of our classes (intro and training level)!

The basic point of this story is that, even when we believe we're using one of the mildest bits around, sometimes it's just not "right" for the horse we're riding. I know, this shouldn't be news to me, and it really isn't, but sometimes it's good to be reminded of the basics. While many horses prefer double-jointed bits because they don't pinch the tongue/poke the roof of the mouth, some horses also don't like the pressure on their tongue that comes from a double-jointed bit. Not rocket science, I know, and not an epiphany, but it's always good to be open to changing our approach.

"I Am a Perfect Rider."

That's right. I am a perfect, faultless, flawless rider, and I'm reminded of that every day when I get onto my flying unicorn. You did get that sarcasm, right? Because the "perfect" rider is right up there with that beautiful flying unicorn. Mythical. Sure, there are many very, *very* good riders, and also some wonderfully naturally talented riders, but none of us are perfect. And it's almost a certainty that the day we smugly congratulate ourselves on how good we are will be the day a horse knocks us down a peg or six. Horses don't care how good or clever you think you are.

And back to those annoying people who have a natural talent for riding. As you can no doubt guess, I'm not one of them, and what skill or ability I have has been earned with blood, sweat, and tears. Sometimes quite literally. I've ridden a lot of "bad" horses; I could often tell which horse I'd be riding for my lesson: usually the one doing handstands in the lesson before mine!

The point of this story is to remind you that there is no perfect rider, and anyone who says they *are* a perfect rider is deluded, a liar, or both. I'm sure even Charlotte Dujardin, with her incredible Olympic dressage scores, feels there are things she can still work on and improve. And I think that's one of the key things about riding horses well. We *never* stop learning, and we also never stop teaching the horse. Every interaction with our horse, we're teaching them something we want them to learn!

We must also make sure we recognize and reward even tiny improvements, whether ridden or handling. For example, my QH mare a few months ago inexplicably began pulling/rushing backward when bridle or halter were removed (and as I'm the one who does that 99 percent of the time, I was confident it wasn't caused by "operator error"). We've been working on it, starting by undoing a cheekpiece to remove the bit and building it up slowly. Last week, she not only stood for bridle removal, but actually dropped her head to make it easier, and she got lots of hugs and loving for that. Now we just need to maintain that return-to-normal routine. I'll leave you with this one thought, which is something I tell all my students: "I don't expect perfection. All I expect is that you strive for it."

Let's Talk about Sex

Okay, okay, so I meant SECS (**s**traightness, **e**nergy, **c**onnection, **s**uppleness). But it made you start reading, didn't it?! SECS are just a few of the many important aspects of riding correctly (but using more/others didn't give me the chance of a fun title for this post).

So, let's start with the most basic, and possibly the most important of the four. Straightness. Which really means correctly bent. If your horse isn't "straight," they can never give you their optimum performance. The old adage was that if you looked down, you should just be able to see the outer edge of your horse's inside nostril. But, of course, straightness actually must involve the whole of your horse's body. And don't underestimate how much your own posture influences the horse's straightness. If you drop your weight more onto one seat bone, your horse will compensate for the shift in weight, thus affecting straightness. You should feel that your horse's hindquarters are moving evenly behind you, their shoulders sitting squarely in front of you, and their head and neck looking nicely central in front of you. Remember to watch the ears. One ear tilted lower than the other indicates a tilted head. If the right ear is low, the nose is off to the left. We could, of course, go on for pages about each element of even this short list, so I'll move on now, but the first key is that we need straightness.

Second comes energy. Now, try not to fall into the trap of mistaking speed, a flat, running trot, for example, for true energy. True energy doesn't mean speed. It means impulsion. It means having our horse moving freely forward into a soft, containing hand. Many times, the first time a rider experiences a "true" working trot, they can be a little unnerved by the power of their horse. I know I was. But a good working trot is a powerful pace. My favorite description is that your legs are acting like a foot on the gas pedal of a car, while your half halts are like tapping lightly on the brake. So, your legs are creating energy, revving up the car, while your hands are preventing any increase in speed. The energy is building up, but being contained and controlled. (Obviously, this description is only really useful if the student also knows how to drive!) So, our horse is now straight and energized. We're halfway there.

Next comes connection. For me, connection is a reminder that a truly round horse is round through their whole body, their whole spine. Connection means that we're *not* focused solely on "headset" (a term which I dislike anyway, because a correctly positioned head is not "set" but should still be relaxed and soft). To me, the head *position* is the last piece of this puzzle we call roundness. A connected horse is one whose whole body is engaged and working correctly. So, the quarters have lowered, enabling the hindlegs to push forward most effectively. My old trainer used to tell us to have the horse "sit down in a chair" under us, to give that feeling of the hindquarters lowering as they drive forward more strongly. The back has raised, as have the shoulders, lifting the horse's weight off their forehand and letting them express the best movement of their forelegs. The neck is gently arched, and the head is down. Remember, though, that a correct outline is *not* having the front of the horse's face on the vertical. A *correct* outline is where the bridle *cheekpieces* are vertical. I would much rather see a connected, engaged horse whose head is a little above the vertical than a horse whose head is perfectly vertical (or often it is behind the vertical) but whose hindquarters are some-where in the next county. Outline comes from behind.

Last but not least, we have suppleness. A supple horse will be relaxed and free-moving, able to show off their paces as we want. And as nature intended. There are no shortcuts to suppleness. Work in your horse properly, incorporating lateral work, transitions, and circles before you worry about outline. If you have your horse straight, energized, connected, and supple, the outline will come all by itself. The big thing about the suppling and warm-up work is that it must be ridden correctly. A half-asleep plod is not a warm-up! Give your horse a few minutes of a relaxed, long rein, yet still a forward-thinking walk, then pick up your rein contact and start to encourage more impulsion. By no means whatsoever is this "all you need to know," and I don't pretend to have all the answers, but these four very basic principles are very important.

Primum Non Nocere

I think that we have a very simple responsibility to our horse. Let's be highfalutin for a second and quote it in the original Latin:

"Primum non nocere."

Okay, no need to run off to Google. It simply means "First, do no harm." And we're not talking about harming your horse physically (though, of course, that is not acceptable either), but that our first responsibility is to work with the horse that we have. Yes, every horse can be trained, but if a horse's heart lies in dressage, neither of you will be happy if you try to make that horse into a barrel racer. So, make sure you're not doing your horse, and yourself, an injustice by trying to make a square peg fit into a round hole.

To be clear, I'm not saying you can't use this hypothetical horse for barrel racing. I'm just saying that it's not their forte, so don't expect them to love it. On the flip side, if your horse's aptitude is for barrel racing or other speedy pursuits, chances are they'll get pretty grouchy if you persist in trying for that perfect fifteen meter circle at a collected canter. Just saying.

I was reading up on social media the other day, and someone had asked people to post any "words of wisdom" that their trainers used as their personal mantra. There were a number of very good comments, and it got me thinking about the things I've been told over the years by my own trainer. I think the biggest thing she drummed into us was straightness. If your horse isn't straight, it can't go forward properly. Seems so simple, yet it can be a real challenge. Particularly when you're working with riding school horses to whom any form of straightness/forwardness/flexion/you-name-it is pretty much a foreign concept at the start. Then, of course, you get into the weirdness of riding in which "straight" actually means "correctly bent." Of course, straightness also applies to the rider. Since the horse will generally move under our weight to support us, if we are sitting with our weight off-center, our horse will be less inclined to be straight. My own particular failing is a habit of "collapsing" my right side, so over the years I have learned to pay attention to the space I can feel between the bottom of my ribcage and the top of my hip bone. If those feel even on both sides, I'm not collapsing my side.

Always remember, doing something wrong isn't a bad thing. The first step to fixing a problem is knowing that it exists. It doesn't matter how often your trainer tells you; until you are able to feel the riding error for yourself, you can't correct it without being told. And often, by the time the trainer sees it and tells you, the crucial moment such as a gentling or releasing of the rein has passed, leading you back into another cycle of work to reach that point once again.

The rider shouldn't create power they can't yet control. There's no point in driving your horse forward with a strong leg if you don't have the softness and acceptance in their mouth to allow you to contain it. When that happens, all you get is a running and unbalanced horse, which I'm pretty sure isn't what we're aiming for! A really simple tip my trainer gave me was to watch my horse's ears. Not to see whether they're pricked, pinned back, flicking, or whatever, but that they're level. If, for example, on a circle your horse's inside ear is a little lower than the outside ear, chances are that their nose is bent to the outside of the circle, even if their body positioning is correct. And always remember, often the best, most sympathetic way to remedy this is *not* to use more inside rein, but more inside *leg*.

Our first duty to our horse, and ourselves, is to make sure we don't mess things up. Try watching your horse move in the field, free, unencumbered by tack or rider. Do they move the same way under saddle? For the moment, let's assume your saddle fits correctly and your horse is wearing the most appropriate bit/noseband. Just by saddling and riding them, we often change how the horse moves. Our aim, particularly for dressage, but really all the time, should be to bring out the horse's natural gaits at their best. So, first, do no harm. You'll never make a horse with an upright shoulder give the same medium or extended trot, for example, that a more sloping shoulder will allow, but your job is to allow the horse to express themselves as naturally and beautifully as their conformation allows.

Of course, we have to work with the horse that we have, and if our affinity is for a particular discipline, then of course we want our horse to do "our thing," which is where choosing the correct horse comes into play. After all, there's no such thing as the perfect horse or the perfect rider. But maybe, if you're very lucky, you'll find the horse that's perfect for you.

Chapter 12

Recommended Reading

There are so many books and websites out there, my real reading recommendation is "as much as possible!" Read everything and make up your own mind, but my personal favorite, go-to books are:

Veterinary Notes for Horse Owners by Horace Hayes
Know Your Horse in Health and Disease by Lt. Col. W. S. Codrington
Horse Nutrition and Feeding by Sarah Pilliner

I also find David Ramey, DVM's website/blog to be very useful and informative (doctorramey.com) as well as pretty amusing, so if you're looking for a down-to-earth vet who is happy to tell you what *not* to waste your money on, give him a read.

Happy riding!

Index